Deterrence & Influence in Counterterrorism

A Component in the War on al Qaeda

Paul K. Davis
Brian Michael Jenkins

Prepared for the Defense Advanced Research Projects Agency

RAND
National Defense Research Institute

The research described in this report was sponsored by the Defense Advanced Research Projects Agency. The research was conducted in RAND's National Defense Research Institute, a federally funded research and development center supported by the Office of the Secretary of Defense, the Joint Staff, the unified commands, and the defense agencies under Contract DASW01-01-C-0004.

Library of Congress Cataloging-in-Publication Data

Davis, Paul K., 1943–
    Deterrence and influence in counterterrorism : a component in the war on
al Qaeda / Paul K. Davis, Brian Michael Jenkins.
      p. cm.
    "MR-1619."
    Includes bibliographical references.
    ISBN 0-8330-3286-0
    1. Terrorism—Prevention. 2. Qaida (Organization) 3. September 11 Terrorist
Attacks, 2001. I. Jenkins, Brian Michael. II.Title.

    HV6431 .D3 2002
    363.3'2—dc21

                                      2002035800

RAND is a nonprofit institution that helps improve policy and decisionmaking through research and analysis. RAND® is a registered trademark. RAND's publications do not necessarily reflect the opinions or policies of its research sponsors.

Cover design by Barbara Angell Caslon

Published 2002 by RAND
1700 Main Street, P.O. Box 2138, Santa Monica, CA 90407-2138
1200 South Hayes Street, Arlington, VA 22202-5050
201 North Craig Street, Suite 202, Pittsburgh, PA 15213-1516
RAND URL: http://www.rand.org/
To order RAND documents or to obtain additional information,
contact Distribution Services: Telephone: (310) 451-7002;
Fax: (310) 451-6915; Email: order@rand.org

This monograph summarizes the findings of a six-month project on deterrence of terrorism, conducted jointly by RAND and the Institute for Defense Analyses (IDA). The project was initiated at the request of Dr. Anthony Tether, the Director of the Defense Advanced Research Projects Agency (DARPA). RAND and IDA worked closely throughout the research and together held two day long seminar/discussion meetings with a senior advisory group. The two organizations, however, developed separate final reports. These were by no means independent, because of the extensive prior interchange, but they provided DARPA with separate "takes" on the issues. The material in this monograph was initially provided to DARPA as an annotated briefing in July 2002, along with accompanying background papers.

The project was sponsored by the Director of DARPA and conducted within the Acquisition and Technology Center of RAND's National Defense Research Institute (NDRI), a federally funded research and development center (FFRDC) for the Office of the Secretary of Defense, the Joint Staff, the defense agencies, and the unified commands. RAND provided research support funds to prepare this report.

Comments may be addressed to Paul K. Davis (pdavis@rand.org), the project leader, or to RAND consultant Brian Jenkins (Brian_Jenkins@rand.org).

CONTENTS

FIGURES AND TABLES

Figures

Tables

PRINCIPLES

This study was initiated by a request to develop a framework for deterring terrorism. It was subsequently broadened to address influence as well, which greatly increased the operating space for our research (Figure S.1), allowing us to consider measures ranging from co-optation to full-scale military attacks executed to deter future terrorist attacks (by al Qaeda or by others).

This broadening of the problem also reflected a lesson gleaned from reviewing historical experience with terrorism: Successful strategies to combat terrorism spawned by serious, deep-rooted problems have involved first crushing the current threat and then bringing about changes to make terrorism's reemergence less likely. Thus, although concepts such as *co-optation* and *inducement* are not effective for dealing with terrorists who have the unshakable commitment of a bin Laden, they *do* apply to others that the United States must try to influence.

It is a mistake to think of influencing al Qaeda as though it were a single entity; rather, the targets of U.S. influence are the many elements of the al Qaeda *system,* which comprises leaders, lieutenants, financiers, logisticians and other facilitators, foot soldiers, recruiters, supporting population segments, and religious or otherwise ideological figures. A particular leader may not be easily deterrable, but other elements of the system (e.g., state supporters or wealthy financiers living the good life while supporting al Qaeda in the shadows) may be. What is

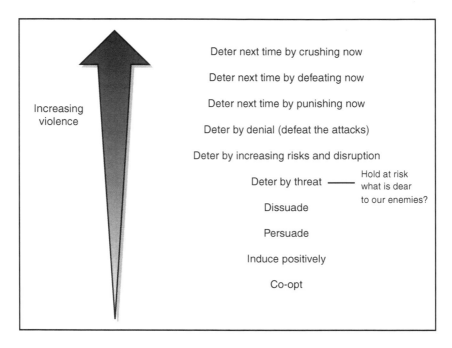

Figure S.1—An Escalation Ladder of the Coerciveness of Influence

needed is a multifaceted strategy that tailors influences to targets within the system. Terrorists are not a uniform group with an on-off switch.

Deterrence, likewise, does not have an on-off switch. Although causing a member of al Qaeda to change his stripes may be out of the question, deterring individuals from attacking individual targets is not. To the contrary, the empirical record shows that even hardened terrorists dislike operational risks and may be deterred by uncertainty and risk. A foot soldier may willingly give his life in a suicide mission, and organizations may be quite willing to sacrifice such pawns, but mission success is very important and leaders are in some ways risk-averse. Terrorists recognize that their power depends on perceptions of whether they are winning or losing; their leaders are deeply concerned with *control*; and martyrdom in a stymied mission lacks the appeal of dying in a spectacular, successful attack.

It is also important to recognize that al Qaeda does not have a single "center of gravity" whose destruction would bring down the whole organization. Nor does the United States have the information that would enable it to pursue such a finely tuned strategy. Consequently, the United States should adopt a broad-front strategy aimed at influencing the many different parts of the al Qaeda system. Where and when the big payoff will occur is a matter for future historians to ponder. This approach is feasible because different organs of government (regular military, special forces, law enforcement, and economic, diplomatic, and political elements) can be employed.

Finally, to sustain its effort for the long term, the United States needs to have and disseminate a persuasive, high-minded strategy, analogous to the Cold War strategy that served the nation so well. Key attributes of that strategy should be:

- Manifest strength and, perhaps even more important, manifest purpose and determination.

- Consistency with American values in war and a moral validity apparent to others with whom the United States needs to work.

- A balance between efforts to crush a particular terrorist organization and efforts to mitigate the factors that give the organization appeal and power (requiring consistent attention by policymakers and those who execute the strategy).

CROSS-CUTTING ISSUES OF STRATEGY

Turning to more specific issues, we conclude that the following challenges are of particular cross-cutting significance.

Orchestrating the Broad-Front Strategy

The campaign to defeat al Qaeda cuts across all of the normal boundaries of war (military, diplomatic, economic, law enforcement, etc.). It needs complex orchestration, requiring simultaneous initiatives at the polar ends of a dichotomy to develop the following:

- *Distributed actions.* Theory, doctrine, rules of thumb, rules of engagement, and information systems are needed to facilitate near-continual distributed decisionmaking and timely, effective action by the diverse elements of the U.S. counterterrorism effort. Timely action is essential because of the distributed, fleeting, and networked nature of the enemy. Centralized command-control is not a good model here.

- *An improved capability for rapid, centralized decisions.* No matter how successful the distributed-decisonmaking effort is, however, some tactical-level decisions that may have profound strategic and political effects will have to be made centrally. Traditional processes for such decisions are likely to be too slow.

Efficiency

Although effectiveness, not efficiency, is most important in war, the United States could defeat itself economically by attempting to do everything everywhere and protect everything too well. Because U.S. vulnerabilities are essentially infinite, the methods of systems analysis, including the influence component, should be applied to the war on terrorism.

Focusing on Adaptiveness, Flexibility, and Robustness

Deterrence depends significantly on convincing organizations such as al Qaeda and those who support it that any notion of defeating the United States—much less "bringing the United States down"—is ridiculous. Although it is unclear whether bin Laden and his associates ever had such grandiose notions, we know that the defeat of the Soviet Union in Afghanistan had a major impact on their thinking. As bin Laden stated in a 1998 interview,[1]

---

[1]John Miller, "Greetings America, My Name Is Osama bin Laden," *Esquire*, February 1, 1999, based on an interview conducted in May 1998 (see *Frontline*, "Hunting for bin Laden," http://www.pbs.org/wgbh/pages/frontline/shows/binladen/, updated September 13, 2001).

There is a lesson to learn from this for he who wishes to learn.
. . . The Soviet Union entered Afghanistan in the last week of
1979, and with Allah's help their flag was folded a few years
later and thrown in the trash, and there was nothing left to
call the Soviet Union.

Even if bin Laden has finite goals, such as causing the United
States to leave Saudi Arabia and back away more generally
from Israel and the Middle East, he has spoken of defeating the
U.S. by hitting its economy,[2] and the zealotry of his agents is
surely enhanced to the extent that the United States is seen as
deeply vulnerable at home. The United States needs to demonstrate that it will not be brought down and will not close itself
down; it must show that it is resilient and will take any
punches, recover, and hit back very hard. Strengthening capabilities in this regard will depend on incentives and standards that encourage modularity, networking, rapid adaptation, and recovery.

TROUBLESOME ISSUES

Weapons of Mass Destruction

A problem of profound concern is the specter of truly catastrophic terrorism involving weapons of mass destruction
(WMD), which some terrorists are eager and willing to use. We
suggest two approaches beyond those already being taken. The
first is to credibly announce that any state or nonstate organization that even *tolerates* the acquisition of WMD by terrorists
within its borders will be subject to the full wrath of the United
States. It must be clear that the United States will lower standards of evidence in ascribing guilt and may violate sovereignty; it may preemptively attack and remove regimes by force.

---

[2]Al Jazeera tape, December 28, 2001, and BBC transcripts, December 27,
2001. Quoted from http://www.truthout.org/docs_01/12.28A.OBL.Vid.Exrpts.
htm: "We say that the end of the United States is imminent, whether bin
Laden or his followers are alive or dead, for the awakening of the Muslim *umma*
(nation) has occurred. . . . It is important to hit the economy [of the United
States], which is the base of its military power."

The relentless U.S. efforts against al Qaeda and the Taliban have helped in this regard, but causing states to turn actively against terrorists in their midst who are involved with WMD presents an additional challenge. Establishing the credibility of a policy that makes tolerance of such terrorist actions intolerable is not easy. Actions will speak louder than words.

The second approach is quite different and controversial:

- Deterrence of the use of biological weapons—a special and frightening case—could be greatly enhanced if everyone in the Middle East believed that such an attack on the United States would inevitably lead to disease spreading into the Middle East, where huge segments of the population would die. A first step would be to encourage recognition of the fact that, because of international travel, infectious diseases such as smallpox would spread rapidly across borders, causing a global pandemic.

Political Warfare

Political warfare is an essential component of any campaign. It should not be confused with the issue of addressing root problems, although that is also a worthy objective; nor should apologies be made for its use. Assuring, for example, that broad-ranging debate occurs within the Middle East (rather than leaving the field to Islamist extremists) is something that can be accomplished in ways that are consistent with American values, including aversion to false propaganda. This subject needs urgent attention.

Placing at Risk What the Terrorists Hold Dear: Convincing Regional Allies to Act

One of the lessons learned from reviewing the ways various influences could be used against the al Qaeda system was that identifying instruments and targets is the easy part. The hard part is making something happen, especially when many of the possible measures would need to be taken by the states from which terrorists come or in which they reside. America's European allies began crackdowns and extensive cooperation with U.S. authorities soon after September 11. Egypt and Pakistan are now doing the same, although Pakistani President Musharraf clearly has major political tensions to deal with.

Saudi Arabia is a special case. On the one hand, the United States and Saudi Arabia have long had a strong strategic relationship. The two countries continue to have shared interests, and Saudi Arabia has even attempted to help resolve the Israeli-Palestinian problem. On the other hand, the spread of religious fundamentalism in the form sometimes characterized by Middle East scholars as "Wahhabiism" constitutes a root problem. It encourages intolerance and can lead to a religious fanaticism that is certainly not intended by the Saudi government, nor is it characteristic of mainstream Islam (which is practiced by many Saudis).

Looking to the future, if influence is to be a meaningful component of counterterrorism, it would seem that the Saudi government will need to do much more than it has done so far to restrain objectionable ideological teachings (and, of course, to impede the support of foreign organizations that in turn support terrorism, a subject already much discussed between the Saudi and U.S. governments).

Balancing *Realpolitik* and Idealism

The United States faces a dilemma in foreign policy. On the one hand, working with current Arab heads of state in Saudi Arabia, Egypt, and elsewhere is very important in the campaign to crack down on elements of the al Qaeda terrorist system. It is also important in pursuing the goal of a Palestinian state and a secure Israel recognized and accepted by its neighbors. On the other hand, maintaining and improving the quality of cooperation will prove difficult if, at the same time, the United States exerts increased pressure to democratize. This dilemma has existed for years and, in practice, the United States has not emphasized democracy as a component of American policy in the region. Many of the region's profound problems, however, including problems of terrorism, are related to the region's lack of democratization. It would be in the U.S. interest to promote open discussion, tolerance, and politically effective compromise rather than violence. The United States has a variety of instruments for this purpose, including increased support of nongovernment organizations (NGOs) attempting to build civil societies. The U.S. State Department could take a number of useful steps if asked to do so. Ultimately, the dilemma is somewhat artificial: It is possible to work with current state leaders and to simultaneously encourage democracy.

Upholding American Values

National standards in war are different from standards in a lengthy peace, but core American values can be preserved in the war on terrorism. On the foreign front, the United States should continue to emphasize being discriminate when using force. It should also demonstrate continued support for democracy even when working with nations lacking qualities that Americans value. Many of America's Western European allies, democracies all, have been forced to change laws and processes to combat terrorism in recent decades. All of them, however, have found it possible to do so without sacrificing their values. The best ways to accomplish such adaptations deserve serious study, with ground rules that permit open-minded rethinking. On a subject such as incarceration, for example, publicity about which has worldwide influence on people's perceptions of the United States, the goal of speedy justice requires due process, but due process does not require the heavy and ponderous machinery that we have become accustomed to in peacetime.

CONCLUDING REMARKS

The concept of deterrence is both too limiting and too naive to be applicable to the war on terrorism. It is important to conceive an *influence* component of strategy that has both a broader range of coercive elements and a range of plausible positives, some of which we know from history are essential for long-term success.

ACKNOWLEDGMENTS

We are indebted to our RAND colleagues who either worked on the project (and participated in many spirited disagreements) or provided useful comments along the way. These include James Dobbins, Bruce Hoffman, Jerrold Green, Laurent Murawiec, Richard Neu, John Parachini, Jonathan Schachter, and Brett Steele. We also appreciate the close collaboration with the project team from the Institute for Defense Analyses—Victor Utgoff (project leader), Brad Roberts, Caroline Ziemke, and Ray Bonoan. Joe Braddock played a key role in conceiving the need for the project and sketching initial ideas. Subsequently, he worked with the RAND and IDA project teams throughout the project.

The project also benefited from an advisory group chaired by General Lawrence Welch (USAF, retired) and James Thomson, presidents of IDA and RAND, respectively. The advisory group consisted of James Schlesinger, General Andrew Goodpaster (USA, retired), the honorable Richard Perle, Leon Sloss, Ted Gold, and Jim Tegnelia.

Finally, we appreciate formal reviews of the draft manuscript by Jerrold Green and Ambassador L. Paul Bremer.

Although we learned a great deal from interactions with our colleagues, the reviewers, and the advisory group, the views presented in this monograph are, of course, our own responsibility.

Chapter One

INTRODUCTION

OBJECTIVES

Our initial goal in this study was to describe a framework for understanding how best to deter terrorists, particularly extremists targeting the United States and its interests.[1] More specifically, we were asked to identify those things that terrorists—in particular, members of al Qaeda—hold dear and, in turn, how the United States could place such things at risk. The work stemmed from a perceived need to supplement ongoing efforts to attack terrorists directly and to defend against their attacks. During the Cold War, the United States benefited greatly from having a well-developed and broadly understood theory of nuclear deterrence, which not only helped guide U.S. planning, but also established a high ground. NATO strategy was also built around concepts of deterrence. Those evolving deterrence concepts were studied and effectively accepted as legitimate throughout the world. Should the United States not have a comparably powerful concept of deterrence for the war on terrorism? After reviewing the issues, we concluded that Cold War deterrence theory was not, in fact, a very good model for our purposes, although it did include several important features that carry over well (see Appendix A). Therefore, we broadened the subject of our research to include influence, rather than deterrence alone.

---

[1]The research was performed in collaboration with the Institute for Defense Analyses (IDA) in a project led by Victor Utgoff (see Bonoan, Davis, Roberts, Utgoff, and Ziemke (2002) for IDA's final report).

APPROACH

The monograph is organized as follows. Chapter Two provides background on the difficulty of deterring terrorism. Chapter Three describes the principles that we found especially helpful in thinking about a broad framework of influence. Chapter Four moves from abstractions to more concrete matters, summarizing cross-cutting challenges of strategy that we concluded are especially important. Chapter Five addresses a series of controversial issues, one by one. Finally, Chapter Six summarizes our conclusions and recommendations and suggests next steps for research. The monograph focuses on particular framework concepts and on troublesome issues, rather than attempting to sketch a comprehensive strategy.

Chapter Two

BACKGROUND: WHY DETERRING TERRORISTS IS SO DIFFICULT

OVERVIEW

This chapter and a companion report (Jenkins, 2002) examine why deterring terrorism is so difficult.[1] The discussion addresses motivations, the mismatch with de facto U.S. policy, the unique characteristics of people involved in terrorist activities, the long-standing traditions of violence within the Greater Middle East, and the fact that terrorists vary greatly in character, which means that no one approach will apply across the board.

The difficulties of dealing with terrorism have not always been apparent to Americans because prior to September 11, 2001, the United States was perceived as virtually invulnerable. The difficulties have been more apparent to America's European allies and, of course, to Israel.

OBSTACLES TO DETERRENCE

Terrorist Motivations Are Strong

However much we may wish it were not so, terrorism has been common throughout history; sometimes, it has even succeeded

---

[1]We have drawn on a large body of RAND work on terrorism. See especially Hoffman (1999) and Lesser, Hoffman, Arquilla, Ronfeldt, and Zanini (1999). A

in bringing about change. To imagine that it could be easily stigmatized out of existence would be both ahistorical and naive. This is especially so when dealing with people who are motivated to employ terrorist tactics because they have no better instruments with which to pursue their aims. Historically, rebellions against real or perceived oppression have *routinely* included the use of terrorism when the rebels did not have the power to succeed otherwise.[2] Although the United States hardly sees al Qaeda and comparable groups as "rebels," some terrorists (e.g., the Palestinians who use terrorist tactics against Israel) see themselves that way.

Terrorism is also difficult to combat because those relying on it may feel they have nothing to lose or because they are motivated by religion or other ideologies in which martyrdom plays an important role. As is now well known, bin Laden and other top leaders of al Qaeda are strongly driven by a particular image of Islam and its crusade against the infidels. Bin Laden may see himself as a prophet or at least as an instrument of God's will.

Nevertheless, some terrorists feel constraints and limit their violence. Unfortunately, the taboo that once existed against mass-casualty attacks may again have disappeared.[3] We say "again" because large-scale rape and pillage of cities is hardly new in history, although the catastrophic potential of nuclear and weaponized biological agents is. History is not encouraging about the prospect of restraining mass-casualty attacks once they become the norm, but taboos have certainly been established and reestablished over time. It is clearly important to reestablish the taboos in our era (see also Chapter Four).

---

larger bibliography is available at www.rand.org/publications/bib/SB2060. pdf. An online source for communitywide bibliographies is http://library.nps. navy.mil/home/terrorism.htm.

[2]See Asprey (1994) and Carr (2002). Our project benefited from a historical review by Brett Steele (unpublished RAND work, 2002).

[3]Roberts (1998).

Deterrence and Eradication Do Not Fit Together Easily

The concept of deterring terrorism also runs into trouble because of a mismatch with U.S. policy. The concept of deterrence, after all, is ordinarily applied in a quid pro quo sense. It is not clear, however, that there is any trade to be made here. Ultimately, the United States is trying to *eradicate* terrorist organizations, and those organizations know it.

Terrorism Is a Way of Life

Deterrence is also difficult because for many of the people involved, terrorism is a way of life. Terrorist organizations may be hurt badly, but those that cause the most concern seldom go out of existence. For one thing, terrorism provides "positives"—notably status, power, recruits, and psychological rewards. More important than this, however, terrorism is the very *raison d'être* of these organizations, so they can can hardly moderate by disavowing it.

Terrorists are not irrational. Some of them, however, operate in an introverted, closed universe and may have a high tolerance for what an outsider would see as drastic conflicts between their professed beliefs about the world and obvious facts.[4]

Traditions of Violence Persist in the Clash of Civilizations

Combating terrorism is not synonymous with destroying al Qaeda or other extremist Islamist groups, but al Qaeda is the major focus today. Unfortunately, many of the most troublesome ideas and behaviors are *not* restricted to extremist groups but apply to a much larger segment of the Arab world (most notably Saudi Arabia and portions of Egypt). Discussion of this issue (see Chapter Five) raises hackles because Americans generally do not wish to tar entire peoples with stereotypical im-

---

[4]Ziemke (2002).

ages. Americans believe fundamentally in universalist concepts such as those underlying the Constitution, concepts also enshrined in the United Nations charter. Nonetheless, there *is* a clash of cultures.[5] Of primary concern is the question of whether this clash can be moderated, channeled, and evolved in benign ways. Denying that it exists will do no good. In particular, Americans believe fervently in religious tolerance, whereas Islamist extremists reject it and embrace violence. Gandhis, they are not. It must also be recognized that portions of the Arab-Islamic world have long lived with traditions in which power is fundamental and violence, including terrorism, is a routine part of gaining and maintaining power.[6,7] When these cultural legacies are combined with social injustice and extreme versions of Islamic fundamentalism, the results are not encouraging: Those who are unhappy may resort to terrorism, including terrorism against "enemies" such as the West, and particularly the United States, on which so much is blamed.[8]

Another consequence of the culture is that terrorists can have compelling reasons *not* to moderate or disband. Leaders who counsel restraint risk accusations of betrayal and even death at the hands of those who feel betrayed. Individuals in an organization may become disillusioned, but in their subculture of fanaticism and violence, they often have no easy way out.

---

[5]See Huntington (1993, 1997) and the responses of his critics, many of them published in *Foreign Affairs*.

[6]See early chapters of Esposito (2002). Although Esposito has written extensively and sympathetically about political developments in the Arab world, the early chapters discuss many of the malign influences at work. Our project also benefited from an unpublished review of such issues by Laurent Murawiec (RAND).

[7]Interestingly, however, a recent survey in the Middle East shows much more widespread respect for democratic concepts within society than has sometimes been claimed in clash-of-civilizations discussions. See Richard Morin, "Islam and Democracy," *Washington Post*, April 28, 2002, p. B05. The survey was conducted by Pippa Norris (Harvard) and Robert Inglehart (University of Michigan).

[8]See Lewis (2002) and Pillar (2001, pp. 29–33) for discussion.

There Is No Single Type of Terrorist

In the Cold War, deterrence operated between two major powers. Terrorism, however, involves many groups, many instruments, and, often, no central command. Terrorists are not a single foe, and no simple theory of deterrence can possibly apply to the spectrum that ranges from anti-U.S. or anti-Israeli "martyrs" to members of American right-wing militias. To make things worse, some of the newer terrorists are not motivated to spare innocents, are more generally uninhibited, and do not calculate thresholds of pain and tolerance in society in the same way that mainstream terrorists of earlier decades did. According to accounts, bin Laden has said[9]

> We—with God's help—call on every Muslim who believes in God and wishes to be rewarded to comply with God's order to kill the Americans and plunder their money wherever and whenever they find it. We also call on Muslim ulema, leaders, youths, and soldiers to launch the raid on Satan's U.S. troops and the devil's supporters allying with them, and to displace those who are behind them so that they may learn a lesson.

> The ruling to kill the Americans and their allies—civilians and military—is an individual duty for every Muslim who can do it in any country in which it is possible to do it, in order to liberate the al-Aqsa Mosque and the holy mosque [Mecca] from their grip, and in order for their armies to move out of all the lands of Islam, defeated and unable to threaten any Muslim.

While in prison, Sheikh Omar Abdul Rahman (the "blind sheikh" who was tried in connection with the 1993 World

---

[9]The full text of bin Laden's February 22, 1998, edict can be found at a Federation of American Scientists web site, http://www.fas.org/irp/world/para/docs/980223-fatwa.htm. See "Jihad Against Jews and Crusaders, World Islamic Front Statement," February 22, 1998. The full English text is given at http://www.fas.org/irp/world/para/docs/980223-fatwa.htm. The original Arabic can be found at http://www.library.cornell.edu/colldev/mideast/fatw2.htm. The quote appeared on the *Frontline* show "Hunting bin Laden," http://www.pbs.org/wgbh/pages/frontline/shows/binladen/

Trade Center attack) issued a *fatwah,* which included the order to

> sink their ships, bring their planes down. Slay them in air, on land, on water . . . kill them wherever you find them.[10]

More recently, Sulemain bu Ghaith, who claims to be a spokesman for al Qaeda, appeared on an al-Neda website and said

> we have the right to fight them by chemical and biological weapons so they catch the fatal and unusual diseases Muslims have caught due to U.S. chemical and biological weapons.[11]

Clearly, when dealing with such individuals, the normal forms of deterrence will not be effective. Moreover, their passionate hatreds are passed on successfully to other people, even to children.[12]

For these and other reasons, deterrence of such messianic terrorist leaders is likely to be difficult. Nonetheless, there are opportunities. The next chapter describes key features of a framework for pursuing deterrence and influence.

---

[10]Bodansky (1999, p. 296).

[11]Fox News, June 10, 2002. Quoted by the Emergency Net News Service, http://www.emergency.com/2001/ter-advsry-sum.htm.

[12]One account describes how youth were motivated by a local Mullah to leave Pakistan and join up with the Taliban. It tells of a village in which 500 young boys were entranced by a spellbinding mullah who claimed that "those who die fighting for God don't die! Those who go on jihad live forever, in paradise." In some cases, at least, their fate could not have been worse. See Jeffrey Gettleman, "Prisoner of Jihad," *Los Angeles Times,* July 21, 2002, p. A.1.

Chapter Three

PRINCIPLES FOR INFLUENCING TERRORISTS

This chapter looks at principles for developing a framework for analyzing deterrence and influence. Most of the principles relate to increasing the range of ways to counter al Qaeda (and terrorism more generally). They deal with (1) broadening the concept of deterrence to encompass influence, (2) approaching terrorist organizations as complex systems, (3) finding situations where influence *may* work (rather than becoming easily discouraged), (4) conducting a broad-front attack, and (5) developing a persuasive, high-minded strategy that can be sustained for years.

GOING BEYOND DETERRENCE

Our study of what terrorists hold dear and how the United States could deter terrorism by placing those things at risk was undertaken to supplement direct military and police actions and defensive measures. However, we concluded that even when we stretched definitions of deterrence, the concept was too narrow to use as an organizing principle. As shown in Figure 3.1, the *influence* component of counterterrorism provides a better framework. The spectrum of influences ranges from co-optation to deterring future actions by crushing terrorists now.[1]

---

[1]Definitions used in this monograph for the terms in Figure 3.1 are given in Appendix B.

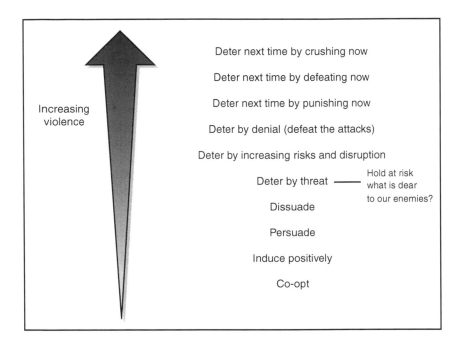

Figure 3.1—An Escalation Ladder of the Coerciveness of Influence

The tactic of crushing terrorists to deter future actions deserves elaboration. Some of the current actions to destroy al Qaeda will contribute to general deterrence later, especially if the United States is seen as strong and *relentless*. Evidence already exists that U.S. efforts against al Qaeda and the Taliban are having such effects on others. After all, what state leader or movement leader today believes that it is wise to take on the United States? Maintaining that attitude should obviously be a priority.[2]

In Figure 3.1, the spectrum is shown as an escalation ladder of increasing violence. This, however, is a Cold War concept that

---

[2]Figure 3.1 is tuned for U.S. purposes. More-repressive states think less in terms of deterrence or influence than in terms of putting their opponents out of business, as illustrated by what has been called coup-proofing in Syria, Iraq, and Egypt (Quinlivan, 1999).

applies poorly here. What is needed today is a *portfolio* of influences—some that are quite coercive and some that include positive inducements. The contents of the portfolio will depend on the target of the influence.

Our emphasis on *influence,* rather than traditional *deterrence,* is derived largely from history, even a quick review of which[3] reminds us how common terrorism has been in both war and rebellion.[4] Our review of history also suggested distinguishing between two classes of terrorists: internalists and externalists, which we shall call Types A and B (Figure 3.2). Over the years, Type A terrorists have ranged from notorious pirates to religious fanatics. However, they are all driven by the action and passion itself. Even when they clothe themselves in ostensible political objectives (as does bin Laden), their appetites for action have proven insatiable and they have changed objectives as necessary to continue.

Type A: self-driven seekers of action, causes, or religious commitment; they may claim political goals, but they are insatiable. Must typically be eradicated, deflected, or isolated.	Type B: terrorists with pragmatic, political world goals; will cease terrorism when it is no longer needed. Must be suppressed; Inducements are needed or terrorism will regenerate.

Focusing *only* on power and toughness can make heroes of Type A terrorists, who otherwise would be repudiated.

The al Qaeda *system* (among others) includes both types, even if al Qaeda itself is clearly Type A.

Figure 3.2—Two Types of Terrorists

---

[3]Unpublished work by Brett Steele (RAND).

[4]Our definition of terrorism includes acts undertaken in war (see Appendix B).

In al Qaeda, one of the most important characteristics of the top leadership is their extremely strong, messianic, religious views. To be sure, al-Qaeda-style Islam bears little relation to more mainstream beliefs and practices, but the fact remains that bin Laden, his top leaders, and many, if not most, of his foot soldiers are *driven* in large part by what they see as their spiritual commitment. Bin Laden probably sees himself as a prophet. The commitment of such people, then, is very different in kind from that of the Palestinian terrorists who have been waging a life-long struggle with Israel.

Extremist spiritual commitment, when embodied in individuals such as bin Laden, lends itself readily to grandiose and unachievable objectives, such as forcing the United States and other elements of "the West" to withdraw from the land of Islam.

In contrast, Type B terrorists have pragmatic, political world goals. They may be equally ruthless and destructive, but they will fade into the "normal world" when they have achieved their aims. Some Type B terrorists end up with honorable positions in society and even in history.

The distinctions are useful, however imperfect, because they have implications for strategy. Type A terrorists, by and large, must be eradicated (in other eras, they might be deflected or isolated). Type B terrorists may need to be firmly suppressed, but because they are often motivated by problems that others also consider legitimate, suppression is not enough; nations must address their concerns (usually in a second phase, after the current terrorist threat has been crushed). This has consistently been necessary both to prevent a new round of terrorism from emerging and because it is ultimately the right thing to do.

In practice, we must deal with a mix of Types A and B. Although al Qaeda leaders are Type A terrorists, many elements of the larger al Qaeda *system* (discussed below) fall into Type B. Enlightened strategy should eradicate the worst of al Qaeda, while not creating martyrs and heroes; it should suppress or otherwise deal with less-violent elements, but it should also include elements of inducement for the longer run. Obviously, "rewarding" terrorism is to be avoided, but at the end of the day, changes should have been made that address some of the root causes of conflict (including inflammatory Islamist teachings). Such changes will not affect the thinking of the bin Ladens of the world, but they may influence the ordinary people who might otherwise join a cause that employs terrorism. All of this seems to be recognized implicitly by current U.S. strategy, which includes both the mailed fist (operations in Afghanistan) and the velvet glove (e.g., attempts to work the Palestinian problem).

VIEWING TERRORIST ORGANIZATIONS AS COMPLEX ADAPTIVE SYSTEMS

A Broad View of System Influences

We use the word *system* in the sense of system framework, systems analysis, systems engineering, or complex adaptive systems. The terrorist problem occurs in a rich context with many interacting entities and processes. Some aspects of the system are hierarchical; others are distributed; still others are networked. Terrorist systems adapt over time (see also Appendix C).

One reason for our system approach is that deterring terrorism is not simply about deterring a single individual or a small group of like-minded individuals (such as the Cold War Soviet Politburo). This is especially so in recent years, as a new class of terrorists has emerged, most notably in the form of al Qaeda. The system phenomenon is more general, however. The Palestinians who are terrorizing Israel are not a single, well-defined group with a well-defined decision process, but rather are members of competing groups that may be seen as parts of a more general uprising.[5] In the future, the United States may be attacked by nonstate actors, such as émigrés with loyalties to their original nation (e.g., Iraq or Serbia). Such attackers

---

[5]See Ziemke (2002); Ziemke, Loustaunau, and Alrich (2000); Shadid (2002); and Esposito (2002).

might or might not be controlled by the state that supports them and might or might not depend on only one or a few leaders.

A second reason for the system approach is that prospects for deterring committed terrorists such as Osama bin Laden or the leaders of other prominent terrorist organizations are poor. (Secretary Rumsfeld referred to such terrorists as "dead-enders.") As indicated in Chapter Two, these people are highly motivated and have already discounted retaliation. Some have nothing that they hold dear *and* that can be easily identified and targeted in a way that would accomplish deterrence. This is not to say that direct deterrence of leaders should not be attempted, but a betting man would favor a broader strategy. Our strategy, then, emphasizes the fact that terrorists in a given group operate within a much larger system, some elements of which are potentially more vulnerable than others. One element of that system is ideology itself.

Decomposing the System into Classes of Actors

Taking a system perspective means, in part, paying attention to the system's constituents. That is, the system must be broken down into parts (i.e., decomposed). Figure 3.3 indicates schematically one such decomposition. In this case, the parts are the different classes of actors—not only leaders, but also lieutenants, foot soldiers, external suppliers and facilitators (e.g., the Arab financiers who support bin Laden while enjoying the good life at home), heads of supportive states, supportive population segments from which terrorist groups draw recruits and within which they find relative sanctuary and physical support, and, finally, other sources of an organization's moral support (e.g., Islamist leaders preaching hate in neighborhood mosques).[6]

---

[6]Initial versions of this decomposition were developed and used by one of the authors (Davis) in a recent study for the National Academy of Sciences (National Research Council, 2002).

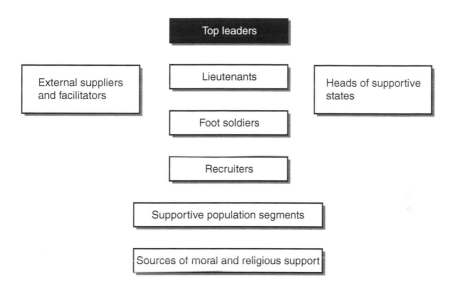

Figure 3.3—The Actors in a Terrorist System

Thinking about whether terrorists can be deterred or otherwise influenced requires such a decomposition. Think about deterring a bin Laden. There are several possibilities to pursue, but killing or incarcerating offers the most promise.[7] However, think next of the contrast between influencing bin Laden and influencing the wealthy Arabs who continue to finance his activities. Bin Laden may feel he has nothing to lose, but at least some of his financiers live comfortably with wealth, family, and prestige. Obviously, they *do* have something to lose. The same is true of most of the actors in a terrorist system, to different degrees and at different times. The segments of society from which the terrorists are drawn may be influenced by international actions and by attacks on terrorist ideology and tactics. Within the United States, those who assist terrorists (e.g., by providing insider information or logistics) may be deterred or

---

[7]Lest we be overinterpreted, even "reckless" leaders can sometimes be deterred at a given time from doing a specific thing. Saddam Hussein was claimed by some to be undeterrable, but he changed behavior drastically when his calculations warranted doing so (Davis, 1997).

apprehended. Finally, the terrorist actors themselves are often concerned about operational risk—they may be willing to risk or give their lives, but not in futile attacks.[8] Thus, better defensive measures can help to deter or deflect, even if they are decidedly imperfect.[9] In Chapter Five we pursue this type of reasoning in more detail to suggest a range of deterrent measures.[10]

Decomposing the System into Classes of Influence

Next, let us consider a different decomposition, one that explicitly identifies different types of influence on the mind of a terrorist or terrorist group contemplating a course of action (Figure 3.4). Here, an arrow from one item to another implies that having more of the first item tends to increase the amount of the second item. For example, the more fear, awe, and sense of futility felt by terrorists as they contemplate the United States (above and to the left of "Deterrence of act" in Figure 3.4), the greater is the deterrence. If the arrow bears a negative sign, it means that more of the first item will mean less of the second. For example, the greater the hatred and blame of the United States and the West felt by the terrorists (below and to the left of "Deterrence of act"), the less is the deterrence. Versions of such influence diagrams have proven useful in a number of disciplines.[11]

---

[8]This is supported by the empirical record of terrorism. See, e.g., Jenkins (2002) and his earlier writings; Roberts (2002); Hoffman (2001); and Lesser, Hoffman, et al. (1999).

[9]A subtlety here is the difference between a defensive system that is imperfect because it has "open doors" and one that is imperfect because it has reliability that is random but much less than one. The first defense might provide no deterrent at all, whereas the second might have substantial effect.

[10]Some of these are drawn from Utgoff and Davis (2002).

[11]The earliest use of the diagrams may have been by Jay Forrester (MIT), the founder of the System Dynamics methodology. Variants called cognitive maps have been used extensively in Britain and by some in the United States (e.g., Axelrod, 1976; Davis, 1997, 2002b).

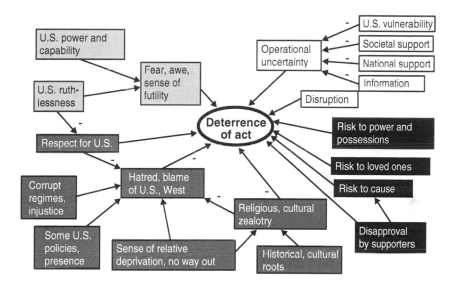

Figure 3.4—A Systemic Perspective

Figure 3.4 has four quadrants. In the upper left-hand quadrant, the influences relate to U.S. power, effectiveness, and perceived ruthlessness. At the upper right, the influences are related to the perception of operational uncertainty and risk. These, in turn, are reduced to the extent that U.S. targets are highly vulnerable, or to the extent that the terrorists receive societal or national support and information. They are increased if the terrorist organization itself is being disrupted. At the lower right, the deterrent influences relate to threats to things the terrorists care about, including their personal power and possessions, loved ones, and their cause itself.

Finally, at the lower left, the influences are related primarily to motivations. A basic problem here is that the support that bin Laden receives has root causes. These create powerful motivations for rebellion, resistance, and even widespread terrorism against innocents. Although bin Laden and many of his lieutenants and agents have not been the victims of poverty or deprivation, tens of millions of people in the region have been. Further, as noted earlier, much of the Middle East suffers from rule by authoritarian leaders, suppression of human rights, and the absence of hope. These people also have convenient alleged villains to blame, ranging from westernization generally to Israel and the United States in particular. Many al Qaeda members and supporters see their actions as pursuing a noble *cause*. Moreover, the combination of historical Arab culture and extreme (but not especially unusual) versions of Islamic fundamentalism appears to provide a structure within which passions can be played out by zealots.[12] Others, however, disagree with this characterization.

Although political, social, and economic factors are among the root causes of problems that foster terrorism, it should also be emphasized that the perverse extremist view of Islam that has been so prominently taught in some Islamist circles is another root cause. Some would argue that it is the most important root cause, since there are countless instances of deprivation in the world that have not led to terrorism.

In thinking about influences, then, there are many levers to work with. Deterrence of some actors depends on many factors, each of which is a potential target for U.S. strategy.

Decomposing the System into a Life-Cycle Perspective

Each decomposition provides a different perspective and, potentially, a different way to conceive strategies and tactics. Suppose, for example, that we consider the life cycle of an Islamist terrorist in the al Qaeda organization as we have seen it operate. Those who hijacked airliners on September 11 for the purpose of attacking the World Trade Center, the Pentagon, and other targets did not come out of nowhere. They were the product of a relatively lengthy process, as suggested in Figure 3.5.[13]

---

[12]See Lewis (2002).

[13]Some of the steps of Figure 3.5 have also occurred in the West. Indeed, the West's open societies can be incubators of radicalism that no one notices until an incident occurs.

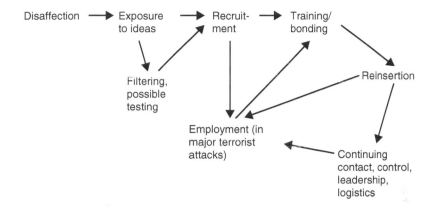

Figure 3.5—The Life-Cycle Process of Individual Terrorists

The individuals represented in Figure 3.5 started out dissatis-
fied in one way or another, not because of economic deprivation
or lack of education, as is sometimes assumed, but for other
reasons. They may have fallen under the influence of peers,
teachers, or Muslim leaders who exposed them to ideas and
activities that they found interesting. They may have been
given minor tasks to do for a still-shadowy organization. At
some point, they were admitted and were sent to training
camps, where they received further inspiration and indoctrina-
tion and bonded with others of similar mindset. They were now
part of something, part of something big. They were then re-
assimilated into society in various ways. In some cases, they
became students. In general, they were admonished to behave
normally and to avoid trouble. There were continued communications and efforts to keep them in the fold, and at some
point they were trained and employed for the big mission. In
the case of the September 11 terrorists, it was also their last
mission—a mission of alleged martyrdom.

We do not know all the details of this life cycle, and it probably
varies across individuals, but the basic picture is correct.
What matters here is that there are numerous places where it
is possible to intervene. The interventions might lead to ar-
rests; or they might disrupt or deter. As a now-familiar example, by destroying training grounds in Afghanistan and putting

nations on notice that similar facilities will not be tolerated on their soil either, the United States is disrupting and possibly dissuading some who would otherwise be hosts. The effort may not be fully effective, but training camps in the jungles of Indonesia may be less troublesome than the continued large-scale operation of the training camps in Afghanistan would have been. As a second example, consider "reinsertion." How are developing terrorist foot soldiers able to reinsert themselves in western civilization? Here, there are many opportunities for action, including tighter monitoring of émigrés and visitors, cooperation with foreign governments to obtain more information about the individuals, and truly integrated databases among organs of government. Such ideas are not new, and related actions are under way in the U.S. government, but viewing them in this structure may provide context and may help explain how the strands of de facto strategy relate to one another.

A Decomposition in the Realm of Ideas

As another example, Figure 3.6 suggests that the willingness of an individual to martyr himself (sometimes in the process of committing murder) probably depends on several subordinate notions. It is at least possible that those notions could be "attacked" in the realm of ideas, whether through the air waves, by influencing the behavior of local Muslim clerics, by firm assertions (and associated actions) by respected Muslim leaders, or by actions against loved ones (see also Chapter Five).[14]

The point of the figure, of course, is again to emphasize that there are many different opportunities for attacking the terrorist system.

---

[14]At a minimum, these actions could prevent the martyr's family from benefiting economically from his action. As has been widely reported, recent Palestinian martyrs have gone to their deaths with the valid expectation that their families would be honored and paid.

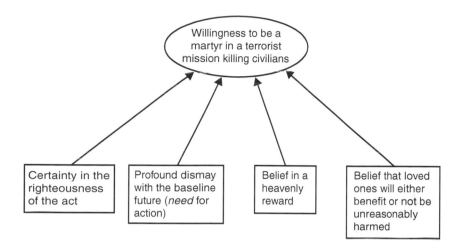

Figure 3.6—A System Decomposition of a Would-Be Martyr's Decision

Other Decompositions

A variety of other system decompositions are useful, depending on the needs of a particular counterterrorist organization. If, for example, we focus on all that is required to accomplish a particular large-scale operation, such as the September 11 attacks or the attack on the USS Cole, we could construct a campaign process (Roberts, 2002), one that would include conceptual planning, initial reconnaissance, initial logistical work, recruiting, training, final logistical preparations, mission rehearsal, and the actual attack.

Yet another decomposition, described previously (Powers, 2001), refers to ideology and value formation; motivation; planning and information gathering; acquisition (of materials and equipment for weapon production); weapons production, deployment, and use; and exploitation.

Again, the idea here is not that one particular decomposition is "right," but that a system perspective, coupled with a variety of decompositions of the system, can provide intellectual and practical frameworks for action. Organizations such as the FBI and the CIA perform such examinations routinely, as do other security organizations, but creating such system decompositions should be an explicit part of counterterrorist doctrine, even for the "soft" subject of deterrence.

FINDING SITUATIONS WHERE INFLUENCING EFFORTS *MAY* WORK

The next principle is to avoid talking in generalities about whether influences will work (the answer will often seem to be "No" when the discussion is too broad), and instead to look specifically for circumstances in which various influences could be brought to bear.

A useful admonition is to always use this syntax: "Under what circumstances might a given effort influence whom, either from doing something or refraining from something?"

Getting beyond "it won't work": Everyone can be influenced sometime.

This may seem obvious, but a great deal of counterterrorism discussion is confused by overaggregation. Can al Qaeda be deterred? Of course not. But wait, what do we mean by that? If we ask, instead, whether elements of the al Qaeda *system* can be deterred from doing specific things, the answer is "Yes." Moreover, even the most dangerous elements in a system may be deflected from one mode of activity to another, or from one set of targets to another. Deterrence and influence are not simple switches.

It is also worth recognizing that even the most dangerous terrorist leaders go through stages, depending on age, successes and failures, opportunities, and associations with others. And even killers can "retire."[15] Thus, we should avoid blanket statements about nondeterrability. Finally, it is virtually a law of social science that people do not behave consistently from one day to the next. Someone who may seem zealous and un-

---

[15]Some examples of this involving Black September and the Irish Republican Army were noted during the project by John Parachini (RAND), who cited earlier work by Hoffman.

bending one day may be "reachable" the next. This is something on which law-enforcement and intelligence agencies have long depended. In practice, "No" may only mean "Not today." Nevertheless, to the extent that bin Laden and other al Qaeda leaders are driven by messianic zeal and a sense of religious mission, retirement seems most unlikely.

When thinking about how to influence whom from doing what, substantial humility is needed: Reliable predictiveness is not likely to exist. Instead, we should get in the habit of thinking in terms of likely outcomes, and also of upside potentials and downside risks.[16]

CONDUCTING A BROAD-FRONT STRATEGY

It is a principle of classical maneuver warfare that a commander should concentrate his resources. Broad-front attacks are often viewed as wasteful and unwise. Far better, it is believed, to find and attack the enemy's "center of gravity." This notion is sometimes sensible and concrete; at other times, it is a form of mysticism. When dealing with some kinds of terrorist organizations, and certainly al Qaeda, the United States has discovered that the beast may have no single head or single heart—there may be no center of gravity to attack.[17] This is not certain. Indeed, bin Laden's death might prove profoundly significant, and the organization might never recover. However, the distributed and networked aspects of the organization (Arquilla and Ronfeldt, 2001), as well as the breadth of its ideological appeal, give us reasons to avoid banking on a center-of-gravity strategy. Instead, the preferred approach is a broad-front attack on all aspects of the terrorist system that are vulnerable. This may be wasteful in one sense, but the stakes are enormous and the alternative is too risky. Further, from an operational perspective, the downside to the broad-front approach is greatly mitigated by the fact that the resources being employed are in many cases different. Military operations are useful for

---

[16]Davis (2001, 2002b). See also Appendix D.

[17]Bodansky (1999, p. 406) warns of this, arguing that bin Laden is only part of a much bigger whole.

some purposes, while vigorous police work (including that of the FBI) is useful in others, so there are different roles for "resources" associated with foreign affairs, economics, ideas, and communications. Although managing the overall counter-terrorist process is proving incredibly complex for many reasons, the virtues and feasibility of the broad-front approach appear to us evident. Indeed, it is what the United States adopted ad hoc shortly after September 11. At that time, there was no preexisting theory, but the theory that emerged appears to us to have been basically correct.[18]

DEVELOPING A PERSUASIVE, HIGH-MINDED STRATEGY

The last of our principles is that the United States, despite having already developed much of a de facto strategy that has served well in the first phase, now needs to develop, articulate, and "sell" a persuasive strategy for the long term. Some of this is under way, but the intellectual framework is still emerging.

This might be a matter of merely academic interest, except for the fact that the struggle with terrorism will probably be of long duration,[19] and this will require a high degree of coherence throughout the layers of U.S. society as well as internationally. It is only natural for people, governments, and businesses to stray from the fold when the immediately visible danger has lessened, other interests intrude, and the "messiness" of counterterrorism is widely seen and deplored. A core reason for NATO's victory in the Cold War was its remarkable commitment (not unwavering, but remarkable nonetheless) (Kugler, 1993).

---

[18]For related discussion about multifront efforts and the challenges of coordination, see Pillar (2001, p. 29 and Ch. 4).

[19]We say "probably" because it is possible that al Qaeda has already been grievously wounded and that within perhaps another year it will prove possible to relax to some degree. Some argue that September 11 may have been a turning point, after which support of extremists such as al Qaeda will wane substantially (Ibrahim, 2002). Currently, we are not sanguine, because of the powerfully negative demographics in the Middle East and the depth of the emotions in that region, many of which are directed against the United States. Further, it currently appears that remnants of al Qaeda remain quite active, even if the organization is still suffering from its major disruption.

If something similar is needed here, and we believe it is, then permanent changes of attitude are needed in legislatures, the intellectual elites, and other groups, not only in the United States, but in other countries, especially those that are the breeding grounds of terrorism.   Thus, however uphill the struggle may be to change some matters, such as the contents of schoolbooks and the sermons given in the local mosques, the effort is worthwhile.

The key attributes of a counterterrorism strategy appear to us to be the following:

*   Manifest strength and, perhaps even more important, manifest purpose and determination.

*   Relentlessness and effectiveness of actions.

*   Consistency with American values and moral validity apparent to others.

*   A balanced mid- and long-term strategy that includes both coercive measures and inducements.

These are necessary for the United States, but not sufficient. The Israelis, for example, have long been strong, purposeful, determined, and relentless, and arguably, they have attempted to maintain moral values and to offer inducements to the Palestinians. Yet their deterrence has not succeeded.

Manifest Strength, Purpose, and Determination

In the war on terrorism, perhaps even more than was the case during the Cold War, it is essential to project a sense of America's strength, purpose, and determination. Its strength has probably been evident enough, but purpose and determination have not. Consider the days before September 11. We believe that September 11 represented a profound failure of deterrence.[20,21] Before the attack, most Americans probably be-

---

[20]Here we draw heavily on material in Schachter (2002).

[21]Others disagree with the conclusion that September 11 was a failure of deterrence due to the appearance of weakness, arguing that the United States

lieved that U.S. strength, purpose, and determination were self-evident (although some of us grumbled about the ineffectiveness of counterterrorism actions in Sudan and Afghanistan). If we take bin Laden at his word—which we believe is reasonable even if we discount somewhat for his propagandistic purposes—a very different image existed in his mind. Consider his statements after the U.S. cruise-missile attack in Afghanistan:

> The American bombardment had only shown that the world is governed by the law of the jungle. That brutal, treacherous attack killed a number of civilian Muslims. As for material damage, it was minimal. By the grace of God, the missiles were ineffective. The raid proved that the American army is going downhill in its morale. Its members are too cowardly and too fearful to meet the young people of Islam face to face.[22]

Consider the score card prior to September 11, as suggested in Table 3.1. In 1983, U.S. forces left Beirut after the successful attack on the Marine barracks. In 1984–1986, the United States made concessions to buy the freedom of hostages in Lebanon. In 1993, the United States withdrew its forces after the Black-Hawk-down incident in Mogadishu. After the attack on the al-Khobar Towers in 1998, there was no obvious U.S. response. When embassies were bombed that same year in Kenya and Tanzania, the response consisted of ineffectual cruise-missile attacks, as mentioned above. There was no visible response to the USS Cole incident in 2000. Finally, of course, came September 11, which did indeed spawn a massive and powerful response, Operation Enduring Freedom. It is not hard to believe, however, that before then, bin Laden and other al Qaeda leaders saw the United States as something that

---

is already believed by many in the Middle East to be strong, determined, and even ruthless. However, its vulnerabilities to homeland attack were objective realities. It simply "made sense" to strike the homeland if the purpose was to change U.S. policy in the Middle East. This was done despite the certainty of retaliation, which might even help al Qaeda's cause if it is seen as an attack on the Muslim world.

[22]"Wrath of God: Osama bin Laden Lashes Out Against the West," *Time*, January 11, 1999; available at http://www.time.com/time/asia/asia/magazine/1999/990111/osama1.html .

Table 3.1

Response to Islamist Terrorist Attacks Prior to September 11

Year	Attack	Overt U.S. Military Response
1983	Beirut	Withdrawal
1984-1986	American hostages in Lebanon	U.S. concessions to buy freedom of hostages
1993	Mogadishu	Withdrawal
1998	Al-Khobar Towers	None
1998	Kenya/Tanzania	Cruise-missile attacks
2000	USS Cole	None

SOURCE: Adapted from Schachter (2002).

could be driven out. Their grandiose interpretation of the Afghan war having brought down the Soviet Union also came into play.

Relentlessness and Effectiveness

It is not sufficient for the United States to have strength and to show determination at a single point in time. Rather, deterrence (and other forms of influence) will be enhanced if the United States conveys clearly that its determination is for the long run, with no respite, no forgetting, and no quarter. Here and elsewhere, we are impressed by the extent to which NATO's Cold War strategy, which combined deterrence with containment, proved appropriate and effective.

The emphasis on strength, determination, and relentlessness is entirely consistent with President Bush's approach. Maintaining the pressure, however, will not be easy.

Consistency with American Values and Moral Validity Apparent to Others

We shall return to this theme in Chapter Five, but it should be a core attribute of U.S. strategy that any actions taken be consistent with American values. Further, the strategy should have a moral validity that is apparent to others who are able to make reasonable assessments. After all, the United States must depend heavily on allies and other international institutions, as well as on other ad hoc nation-to-nation arrangements.

A historical rule of thumb here has been to maintain discrimination in the use of force. Although critics of the United States are quick to remember the firebombings and nuclear weapons of World War II, the long-term norm of U.S. behavior in war has been the discriminate use of force.

Balanced Strategy

Finally, strategy should have parallel components. As mentioned at the outset, history strongly suggests that the United States must seek simultaneously to crush al Qaeda *and* to address sources of unrest. History also suggests that the crushing phase should be accomplished first (in part to avoid encouraging terrorism), but the groundwork for the more positive features must be begun early if the strategy is to bear fruit later.

To reiterate, there is no doubt that the United States must crush al Qaeda, while taking care not to make its members into heroes. In this task of eradication, "deterrence" is a mere tactic. This is not controversial. To succeed in the long run, however, the United States must address root causes or a next generation of terrorists will emerge. In our view, the *principal* root cause of today's terrorism is the virulent form of Islam adopted by al Qaeda.[23] It must be defeated. In addition, however, we unabashedly acknowledge that some of bin Laden's supporters have legitimate concerns. Their grievances are ill-posed, self-serving, and dysfunctional (as when Islamists blame

---

[23]Ambassador Bremer said some years ago, "There's no point in addressing the so-called root causes of bin Laden's despair with us. We are the root cause of his terrorism. He doesn't like America. He doesn't like our society. He doesn't like what we stand for. He doesn't like our values. And short of the United States going out of existence, there's no way to deal with the root cause of his terrorism" (Bremer, 1998).

the West and the United States for the plight of Islamic states in the Middle East), but their problems exist nonetheless.

Developing a balanced strategy is necessary, but its execution will remain extremely difficult. We need look no further than the current (2002) Israeli dilemma of how to deal with Palestinian suicide bombers to appreciate the problem. It is easy to deplore Israeli tactics in the West Bank (e.g., the razing of buildings and neighborhoods or the deporting of terrorists' family members),[24] but precisely what alternatives suggest themselves in the current environment?

---

[24]A recent tactic, a crude assassination by bombing that killed many civilian Palestinians, does not fit in this list. It was beyond the pale and was deplored by President Bush and other world leaders.

Chapter Four

BROAD ISSUES OF STRATEGY

In this chapter, we discuss certain cross-cutting considerations that should play a major role in U.S. counterterrorism strategy, including its influence component. They are not so much controversial as they are unappreciated (controversial topics are the subject of Chapter Five). The items we mention here relate to counterterrorism strategy generally, not just to influence.

ORCHESTRATING A BROAD-FRONT STRATEGY

As mentioned in the previous chapter, the war on al Qaeda should be a deliberate broad-front attack. It is already that in practice, but the rationale for sustaining this approach is less established and troubles are certain because such a strategy requires relating the efforts of multiple agencies, subagencies, and even nations, and it sometimes necessitates rapid action. This would seem to require *two* enhancements of capability which may at first seem contradictory, but they are complementary and equally important.

Improving the Capacity for Effective Distributed Decisionmaking and Action

International terrorism involves what some refer to as netwar: The enemy is highly distributed, makes good use of semi-autonomous cells, and encourages local entrepreneurial actions, rather than demanding central control of all actions. In addition, targets for counterterrorism actions are often fleeting, as are opportunities to attack preemptively or take other special defensive measures.

> Timely, sound actions by distributed actors will require sophisticated doctrine and nuanced rules of engagement.

All of this suggests the need for near-continual, distributed decisionmaking and procedures that allow timely actions. The agent on the street, the company commander in the field, the diplomat seeking to bring influence to bear, and the operative seeking to influence public opinion in the Middle East will need to be able to act promptly, based on information available from many sources. To put it differently, defeating networked terrorists probably requires sophisticated netwar in response.[1] That, in turn, is much more than a matter of linking databases and assuring communications. To wage netwar properly will require that those who are empowered operate under a theory, a set of principles, and a doctrine that is readily understood and disseminated. This should include rules of engagement and an understanding of higher-level issues and tradeoffs permitting rapid adaptation by actors on the scene. Such discipline must be revisited and reinstilled because the pressures of action operate against it.

Although the analogy is imperfect, the United States has relevant experiences. Some have been positive, while others have been sobering and cautionary. U.S. Special Forces units, for example, have often been given a great deal of autonomy and license. They have been expected to make nuanced calls and to avoid serious and visible blunders that would have higher-level ramifications. For the most part, they have been successful, largely because the personnel in these units are chosen for intelligence as well as physical prowess and are trained to understand well the context of their missions. There have also been very positive examples of special police antigang units. In contrast, there have been many examples of military or law-enforcement units (including other antigang units) that have been given a great deal of autonomy and have then run amok. In summary, the kinds of distributed fast-acting capability

---

[1]See Arquilla and Ronfeldt (2001).

needed may be clear enough, but achieving them is not straightforward and should begin with what might be broadly called doctrine.

Improving the Capacity for Rapid Centralized Decisions

The value of distributed operations is apparent throughout the American economy and does not need to be defended so much as encouraged.   Nonetheless, even with superbly networked counterterrorism forces that have first-rate doctrine for on-the-scene decisionmaking and action, there will also be a need for some decisions to be kicked to central authorities and for those authorities to orient, assess, and decide on actions quickly. The "tactical" actions contemplated will have strategic implications and will simply not be candidates for local initiative.[2]

In the war on terrorism, many of the issues involved will be more like those of grand strategy than those of purely military matters.   The United States, for example, cannot violate sovereignty lightly in pursuit of terrorists or in preemptive actions.   Such actions may well be ordered, as President Bush has hinted on more than one occasion, but they will not be taken lightly and they will be decided by central authorities who can see across political, military, and economic boundaries and who can orchestrate actions with other nations and agencies.

Decisions of this type are already being made, with committees of deputies as the common mechanism for debate and decision. However, if it is believed that there will be a need for rapid decisionmaking and complex orchestration of actions, then such business-as-usual committee approaches will not suffice.   Two examples are illustrative: The first is the U.S. cruise-missile

---

[2]It is instructive to observe that commanders in chief (CINCs), now called combatant commanders, or their deputies have often found it necessary to make tactical-level or even engagement-level decisions in recent military operations, such as those in the Balkans, precisely because "small events" can have strategic consequences.   It is not that the commanders in question *wanted* to micromanage.

strike against a training camp in Afghanistan, which came too late. An assembly of important al Qaeda figures had met there, but they had dispersed by the time the missiles struck. The second example is the missed opportunity to strike bin Laden and his associates with a drone-mounted missile operated by the CIA. In this case, one might argue that there "should" have been better rules of engagement, but there will always be surprises for which prior thinking proves to have been inadequate, and these will require central decisionmaking.

In such cases, there will be a need for an improved form of continual staffing and rapid decisionmaking, even by dispersed high officials, including the President. The political challenges involved are, of course, enormous. So also are the technological challenges, since there is no good precedent as yet. Indeed, the history of decision-support systems for complex strategic-level work is not encouraging, and we therefore believe that it will be necessary to have competitive approaches and an unusual emphasis on assuring that results add value to the hypothesized orchestration group.[3]

It might even be asked here whether the war on al Qaeda should be run not by a region-focused CINC, but by a full-time, round-the-clock task force dedicated to this mission and looking at all relevant information worldwide. It is beyond the scope of our work to make proposals on this issue, but at least two very different models suggest themselves for analysis. The first would be to have the task force report directly to the National Security Council, which would have the advantage of emphasizing the cross-agency, grand-strategy aspects of the challenge. It would have the disadvantage of not having a home in an agency experienced in operations. The second model would have the task force be more like a global analog to a regional CINC, but reporting to the Secretary of Defense and the Chairman of the Joint Chiefs. It would have substantial

---

[3]DARPA is currently conducting research on advanced versions of decision support that will include extensive networking and will enable some of what we have in mind. Over the past decade, considerable progress has also been made within the executive branch in bringing about cross-agency political and strategic-level work (Hawley, 2002).

support from the non-Department of Defense (DoD) agencies and one or more deputy "commanders" from such agencies to assure the appropriate balance of discussion and decision.

Relationship to the Influence Component of Counterterrorism

The examples above related primarily to direct actions; analogous issues also arise within the influence component of U.S. strategy. Indeed, the distinction between direct actions and influencing actions is often blurred in practice because a given action may have both direct and indirect effects (a theme of so-called effects-based operations, as described in Appendix D). For example:

- Decisions to engage ambiguous targets on the battlefield may have profound effects on attitudes toward the United States, ranging from enhanced appreciation of U.S. power and determination to bitterness about attacks on innocents.

- Decisions to encourage allied actions against extremist religious schools and individual Islamic-cleric firebrands probably need to be made locally but they should be informed by broader policies.

- Some domestic law-enforcement actions might have to be initiated immediately for effectiveness but could be perceived as the actions of "jack-booted feds" if they are not orchestrated with local authorities and political figures.

- The extreme disruption of air travel resulting from mandated evacuation of facilities creates major vulnerabilities to terrorist false-alarm tactics; more local discretion is needed, but the analog to rules of engagement is also needed.

A much larger issue here is how the U.S. government should approach the concept of terrorism and the communication of threat. The more extreme the disruption that terrorists regard as plausible, the weaker is deterrence. This has major ramifications for how the general threat of terrorism is framed and how more-specific threats are communicated. As a consequence of September 11, the United States is already spending about $100 billion for homeland security (on the public, private, federal, and local levels). The indirect consequences on the economy probably increase this figure to several hundreds of billions annually.

THE STRATEGIC SIGNIFICANCE OF EFFICIENCY, EVEN IN WAR

A second cross-cutting challenge relates to efficiency. We are not especially interested in efficiency on the battlefield—effectiveness is good enough. However, aspects of counterterrorism must necessarily be efficient, because U.S. internal vulnerabilities are essentially infinite. Current political requirements call for 100 percent screening of airline passengers and baggage, but such comprehensive approaches are infeasible for the nation's activities as a whole. This suggests the need for DoD-style analysis—in particular, portfolio-management analysis—to allocate resources wisely and to assure focus and coherence in "strategy-to-tasks" work (such work is, of course, consistent with the thrust of the new Homeland Defense Strategy). The same can be said of allocating resources for the influence war abroad.[4] Even with a broad-front strategy, there are too many possibilities and too few trained people to do everything everywhere.

Another consideration here is that overzealousness in protective measures creates enormous vulnerability to terrorists even if those terrorists lack competence: The mere threat of attack or half-baked efforts that end in capture can drive the United States to greater and greater expenditures that can only be considered overhead expense. This, we believe, is a major economic problem that has not yet been addressed well. The United States appears to still be in a phase in which citizens

---

[4]The need for such methods is referred to also in National Research Council (2002). See Hillestad and Davis (1997) for a portfolio-management tool that has been used in a number of defense and nondefense applications. The Air Force and the Joint Staff have implemented versions of the strategies-to-task methodology, originally developed by Glenn Kent and others (see, e.g., Lewis and Roll, 1993).

and political leaders are demanding ever-higher levels of protection, with little discussion of the tradeoffs.

A PARADIGM FOR DEFENSE

The third cross-cutting challenge relates to the necessity to depend upon adaptation and recovery in defense. This, in turn, leads to the need for improved modularity and so-called "capabilities-based planning," rather than "scenario-based planning." That is, it is necessary to develop broad wherewithal to cope with diverse circumstances, rather than finetuning plans based on specific scenarios. The goal is to have flexible, adaptive, and robust capabilities, rather than capabilities designed for a particular scenario that assumes a specific enemy; specific circumstances of warning time, allies, and enemy and friendly strategies; and specific national objectives.[5] Achieving such capabilities is notoriously complex. It requires a passion for adaptiveness and substantial analysis leading to a combination of incentives, standards, and policies.

Aside from their direct value for defense per se, such preparations and their exercise could contribute significantly to deterrence by helping to dispel any notion that the United States can be easily toppled. Recovery from the attacks of September 11 was remarkable and gratifying to Americans, but the message sent to al Qaeda may have been different from the one intended. Newspaper accounts pointed out that the attack on the Pentagon would have had a much greater effect had it struck another side of the building; the entire airline system was temporarily brought to a halt; recovery expenses and indirect consequences will cost hundreds of billions of dollars. And, of course, the presumably unrelated anthrax letters had a massive effect on the U.S. Senate and much of the federal government.

---

[5]The reasons for capabilities-based planning are discussed in Rumsfeld (2001). A more detailed discussion of analytical implications is given in Davis (2002a), and an earlier treatment is given in Davis (1994).

For more than a decade, U.S. economic growth has been driven in directions (e.g., toward just-in-time scheduling) that in some respects create vulnerabilities and the potential for major disruptions from which it would be difficult to recover. To be sure, not all the trends have gone in this direction—in particular, the infrastructure for networking has improved the situation a great deal. Nonetheless, major studies are needed on how best to modify economic and other incentives so as to encourage more adaptive and recoverable systems. One goal of the information campaign should be to communicate a sense of that American capacity to adapt and recover. No terrorist leader should be easily able to imagine that the United States can be brought down by a few discrete attacks of a sort that he might bring about. The key point is that

• Some deterrence can be achieved by demonstrating that terrorist attacks will not bring the United States down or cause it to close itself down and that the nation is able to take the punches, recover, and hit back very hard.

Deterrence depends heavily on this, but the United States is still giving the impression that it is closing itself down to a considerable extent, which in turn gives terrorists enormously more power. There may be lessons here from the experiences of others, such as the British, who had to deal with Irish Republican Army terrorism in London and who did so with only modest disruption, and the Israelis, who have for many years dealt with chronic terrorism. The current rash of suicide bombings is in part testimony to Israeli successes with less-violent forms of terrorism.

Chapter Five

SOME CONTROVERSIAL ISSUES

In this chapter we address a discrete set of controversial topics: (1) deterring acquisition and use of weapons of mass destruction[1] (WMD); (2) political warfare; (3) threatening the things that the terrorists hold dear; (4) challenges in U.S.-Saudi relations; (5) the Pakistan problem; (6) balancing U.S. interests in enlisting regional allies, maintaining stability, and promoting democracy; and (7) the feasibility of maintaining American values during a war against al Qaeda.

DETERRING ACQUISITION AND USE OF WEAPONS OF MASS DESTRUCTION

Deterring acquisition and use of WMD is profoundly important and difficult. Terrorists appear to have grandiose intentions, and some have intense interest in such weapons. Moreover, they may believe that they have what a Cold War theorist would call "escalation dominance." That is, al Qaeda could use WMD against the United States, but retaliation—and certainly escalation—would be difficult because (1) the United States will not use chemical, biological, or radiological weapons; (2) its nuclear weapons will seldom be suitable for use; and (3) there are no good targets (the terrorists themselves fade into the woodwork). And, of course, the United States has constraints. Although

---

[1]Some observers refer to these as mass-*casualty* or mass-*disruption* weapons, believing that even major terrorist efforts are more likely to cause casualties and massive disruption than mass destruction.

this gap in the deterrent framework is dismissed by some, we regard it as very dangerous.

We see two approaches: (1) threatening anyone who even tolerates WMD-related terrorism, and (2) deterring biological weapons.

Threatening Anyone Who Even Tolerates WMD-Related Terrorism

The United States could announce credibly that the response to WMD would be powerful and would be sustained (for as long as necessary). It could make clear that the United States would violate sovereignty and preemptively attack as necessary, deep into other nations, and that it would act upon "reasonable" evidence and would even make some assumptions about who is supporting terrorists in possession of WMD. Further, it would punish not only active supporters, but even those states and factions that merely tolerate the terrorists or indirectly facilitate their acquisition of WMD. The purpose would be to so alarm heads of state and heads of substate organizations that they would work actively to get rid of elements that might bring destruction down upon them.[2]

The credibility of such announcements has improved in the wake of Operation Enduring Freedom in Afghanistan. Despite the criticisms of President Bush's "axis-of-evil" comments, the heads of state of Iran, Iraq, and North Korea know that they have been put on notice. Actions will speak more loudly than words, however.

Critics of this approach say that the United States has already declared this level of retaliation, since al Qaeda has already crossed an unacceptable line. Thus, what threat still remains that can be used for deterrence? Such criticism misses the point: The target here is not al Qaeda or the Taliban, but the

---

[2]John Parachini (RAND) has discussed such issues in terms of the necessity to broaden and deepen the red line that seems to have operated in the past. So far, relatively few states have been known to be cooperating with terrorist organizations in acquiring WMD.

states and substate groups that might aid or tolerate such organizations. Deterring them is a continuing problem. Deterrence is probably operating now to a substantial degree. What state *today* would emulate the Taliban? Unfortunately, such deterrence will fade unless it is continually renewed.

Deterring Biological Weapons

Deterring biological weapons is especially controversial—it was controversial even within our own research team and among colleagues with whom we consulted in the course of this research.

The Problem. The single kind of act against which deterrence is most important is mass-casualty attack, e.g., attack using radiological, biological, or nuclear weapons. It seems clear that some terrorist leaders would use such weapons if they could do so and that others are seeking weapons with related capabilities. Furthermore, many people in some countries would probably cheer if the target were the United States or Israel. Because some such weapons will almost surely fall into terrorists' hands at some point, and because foolproof defense is very unlikely to exist, it is crucial that attitudes be hardened against their use. How might this be done?

The United States could attempt to incite certain attitudes within the terrorist systems, such as:

- Moral repugnance.

- Fear of backlash from supporting populations.

- Fear of mass-casualty retaliation or the passive spreading of disease.

The first two items create challenges but no dilemmas. If the United States can stimulate clerics and other respected figures to speak strongly and consistently against the immorality of mass-casualty weapons, it should certainly do so. The last item, however, does raise a dilemma. It is worrisome, especially to those who believe that fear is often a better deterrent than appeals to morality, because no such fear of mass-casualty retaliation seems to exist today. The absence of such fear must increase substantially the likelihood that terrorists will actually use mass-casualty weapons if they can do so. The dilemma arises in determining how the United States might go about stimulating that fear.

Ironically, it would be only logical for would-be users of mass-casualty weapons to be *very* concerned about retaliation. If they believe their own rhetoric, they should also

- See the U.S. firebombing of Japanese cities in World War II and the subsequent A-bombing as clear evidence of U.S. willingness to use mass-casualty weapons if aroused.

- See the deaths of Iraqi innocents resulting from western-imposed sanctions as a more recent example of determined ruthlessness toward Arabs and Muslims.

- See violent retaliation from Israel or its Mossad as a constant threat by a state capable of anything.

Polls indicate that vast numbers of people in the Middle East erroneously believe that Israel was responsible for the September 11 attacks on the World Trade Center and the Pentagon, and that there was a massacre at Jenin. Should they not logically be concerned, then, that Israel would resort to mass-casualty weapons if that Pandora's box were opened? Even though the actual perpetrators of September 11 know full well who was responsible, and even though Palestinian leaders may know that no massacre occurred in Jenin, their supporters may not.

These speculations are "passive"; that is, they refer to ways terrorists might be self-deterred. However, counting entirely on self-deterrence would be folly. We must ask what the United States and its allies should do to improve deterrence with respect to mass-casualty weapons, especially if we doubt the sufficiency of appeals to western concepts of morality.

A Modest Proposal. This suggests the following as a high-priority initiative:

- Attempt to influence opinion-molders in the Middle East to write and talk at length about the horrific dangers to the Arab Middle East if the United States, Israel, or other western countries were to be struck with mass-casualty weapons.

The ideal article or speech on the matter would note that in recent wars the United States has gone to great lengths to avoid unnecessary civilian casualties, but it would then recount past examples of mass casualties (e.g., by firebombing, A-bombing, city attacks in Vietnam, etc.) where the United States deemed the actions necessary. It would go on to discuss the Pandora's box problem, argue that history tells us that retaliation would be inevitable sooner or later (despite current U.S. rejection of mass-casualty weapons), and observe that poor people in the Middle East would be *extremely* vulnerable because of the lack of medical services. It would also observe that whole populations have been decimated by smallpox, plague, and other diseases that spread rapidly even if no one wants them to do so.[3] The story would be accompanied by graphic visuals. Finally, such a discussion might review the development of the Israeli nuclear program and apocalyptic options ascribed to it.[4]

The ideal would assuredly not be attained. Any articles or speeches would probably be extremely critical of the United States—but perhaps no more so than is already the norm in such matters. Discussion might further increase the impression that some Middle Easterners have of U.S. callousness. Arguably, however, the only thing that would matter is the effectiveness of the story in raising the level of fear and thus creating pressures by supporting populations, state supporters, and perhaps even terrorist lieutenants and leaders to avoid mass-casualty attacks. The question has been asked, What do these people hold dear, and how do we place it at risk? At least

---

[3]The United States could simultaneously encourage increased international efforts to improve public health against infectious diseases, thus underscoring the fact that global health is a universal goal upon which any biological attack would be an assault.

[4]For a journalist's account, see Hersh (1993).

some of the terrorist leaders and supporters almost surely hold dear their families, tribes, homes, and people.

A rejoinder to the suggestion might be the question, How would the United States arrange for influential opinion-molders to write what it wants? In fact, intelligence agencies have considerable experience in handling such challenges covertly, e.g., with secret leaks and side payments. However, there is no evident need for such covertness. Regardless of who brought the issue forward for open discussion (even a senior U.S. official or some other person who would be of interest to the Arab-world media), and even if the news media people dislike the United States intensely, the facts would be so powerful that the intended result might be achieved. We, at least, believe that the story is basically correct: Retaliation *would* occur somehow, however unimaginable that may now seem and however immoral employment of mass-casualty weapons may be.[5]

A worry might be that the media in question would go on to invent plots, such as that the CIA or Mossad was already developing and planning offensive use of mass-casualty weapons. The recently publicized government efforts to study biological warfare again would probably be referred to as indication of offensive intent. Perhaps the outrageous claim of CIA complicity in the AIDS epidemic would be revived. Nonetheless, the value of creating (or rekindling) fear about mass-casualty retaliation might be worth the risk. Although this point is quite controversial, we believe that the U.S. government should examine this issue directly, rather than nibbling at the edges, e.g., advertising the point that some biological weapons would have unintended consequences because people infected with the disease would travel—including to the Middle East—before

---

[5]A partial analog here involves the long-term effort by both American and Soviet governments to warn everyone about the *potential* uncontrollability of nuclear warfare. It is not that either side's leaders lacked determination to attempt control; rather, they realized both that controllability might not be possible and that, in any case, highlighting this fear contributed to deterrence.

being diagnosed. Such a ploy would avoid dealing with the principal issues and would merely encourage terrorists to avoid one of the least likely instruments.

The ramifications of any such effort would be large. Thus,

- The U.S. government should conduct research on how best to proceed with this initiative. Research should include human games and focus groups with well-selected participants who could shed light on likely and possible reactions to different tactics by different types of individuals in the Middle East and elsewhere. It could include modeling of potential indirect and cascading effects, as in so-called effects-based operations.[6]

Alternatives. What else might be done? The United States might actually develop and announce (or leak information about) appropriate weapons of and doctrine for retaliation with mass-casualty biological or radiological weapons. It could be argued that doing so would be no more immoral or unthinkable than the core of nuclear deterrence during the Cold War. We recommend against such measures for at least two reasons. First, by preparing such weapons, the United States would almost surely lose some of its moral authority and cohesiveness, both domestically and internationally. Second, there seems no need for advance preparation. Even if it were decided that retaliatory attacks with chemical or biological weapons were needed, developing the options would probably not be especially difficult or prolonged. More important, area attacks with conventional or even nuclear weapons could be mounted at any time. It would seem, then, that this particular moral dilemma can be avoided for now. The problem is not U.S. capability, but the apparent absence of fear on the part of some terrorist groups.

---

[6]For an overview, including criticism of hype and cautions, see Davis (2001).

POLITICAL WARFARE: THE NEGLECTED COMPONENT OF ANTITERRORISM STRATEGY

Political warfare relates to what is sometimes referred to as the war of information and ideas. We find it striking that political warfare is so obviously missing in the current effort. It is not that no one has noticed, but rather that the United States has still not gotten its act together on this matter. Political warfare has always been a standard component of warfare, for which no apologies are needed. This is not the same as addressing root problems or "affecting hearts and minds," however desirable those activities are. Even if one takes the view that America's enemies in the Middle East hate the United States, will always hate the United States, and are untouchable by logic, persuasion, or amelioration of problems, political warfare is essential.

It is important to emphasize that political warfare need not be inconsistent with American values in war. Obviously, in the war on terrorism, measures are being used that go beyond what is normal, but these are not ordinary times. As in many past wars, and as has been recognized by all of America's European allies when they were the victims of terrorism, laws and practices must be adapted. Nonetheless, this does not imply an abdication of basic values.

As one example of political warfare, consider the fact that in some parts of the Middle East, the dominance of Islam, even fundamentalist Islam, cannot be effectively challenged. But it is in the U.S. interest to encourage debate, because the baseline of beliefs is so malign and so antithetical to U.S. values and interests that opening the discussion up is almost certain to move the center in a favorable direction.

How can this be done? This is a subject for research and experimentation, but it is a classic challenge of political warfare. During the 1950s, for example, "democracy was saved" in Italy in part because noncommunist political ideas and political candidates had suitable visibility and funding and in part due

to covert efforts of the CIA.   Today's activities would be different, especially in the Middle East and because of the emergence
of the Internet, but the challenge would be similar.[7]

PUTTING AT RISK WHAT THE TERRORISTS HOLD DEAR

Let us next consider the question, How does the U.S. hold at
risk the things the terrorists hold dear?

The system approach we have adopted helps by identifying options, often including built-in escalation ladders.   Table 5.1
provides a summary.[8]   The table is arranged more or less in
parallel with the decomposition of the terrorist system into the
types of actors introduced in Chapter Two.   The right-hand col-
umn lists influence measures that could be brought to bear on
the different actors.

Although straightforward deterrence of terrorist leaders is difficult, much can be done to deter them from some actions.   As
mentioned above, these people often mistrust and fight among
each other, disagree, and vary in conviction.[9]   It should be
possible, then, to turn them against each other by disinforma-
tion and deception.   It may also be possible to convince them
that their particular actions ultimately work *against* their
cause.   And, as noted in Chapter Two, raising operational risks
can deter certain activities.

Many have suggested threatening the terrorists' families, as
though that were a straightforward and moral thing to do.   This

---

[7]The Bush administration is apparently planning to open an office of global
communications in the near future.   See Karen DeYoung, "Bush to Create
Formal Office to Shape U.S. Image Abroad," *Washington Post*, July 30, 2002,
p. A1.

[8]This draws on a briefing by Utgoff and Davis, "Toward a Strategy for Deterring
Terrorism," which is included in Bonoan, Davis, Roberts, Utgoff, and Ziemke
(2002) along with more extensive suggestions along the same lines.

[9]A fascinating glimpse at the kind of people we are discussing and their
internal battles, deceptions, and motivations is provided by Higgins and
Cullison (2002), which pieces together information on Ayman al-Zawahiri.

Table 5.1

Threatening What the Terrorists and Their Supporters Hold Dear

Participants in Terrorism and What They Hold Dear	What the United States Might Do
Leaders	
Power	Turn leaders against each other (by disinformation, deception).
Cause	Convince them that attacking the United States undermines their cause; raise operational risks.
Family, tribe, brotherhood	Cause state leaders to prevent rewards to families of terrorists and even to punish them by withholding privileges; cause state leaders to harass terrorist leaders and punish them economically.
Foot soldiers	
Cause; excitement	Raise operational risks; with continuing U.S. successes, both micro and macro, demonstrate the folly of the cause's path.
Family, tribe, brotherhood	See above.
Financiers, etc.	
Cause	Discredit their cause within Islam and society.
Wealth, power, life	Cause loss of wealth, prison, death, and dishonor.
Family, tribe, brotherhood	See above.
Logisticians	Cause prison, death, and dishonor.
State supporters	
Power	Selected strikes and incursions (preemption); impose military, political, and economic sanctions; shun supporters of terrorism.
Own political goals	Convince them that attacks on the United States undermine their cause; provide other ways to seek goals.
Populations	
Survival	Provide hope (peace process, aid, liberalization, etc.).
Bitterness, blame	Broaden the range of ideas and views discussed.
Cause	Remind them "who rides the bigger horse" (cite U.S. successes against al Qaeda, local suppression).
Religious leaders	
Power, status	Trump (discredit them), warn them off, monitor them, shut off funds.
Personal and family welfare	Cause prison, death, and dishonor, and prevent benefits to families.

NOTE: See also the more-extensive discussion in Bonoan, Davis, Roberts, Utgoff, and Ziemke (2002).

is arguably not the case, but there are things that can be done. At a minimum, the families of terrorists should not be rewarded, as they commonly are today. Escalating, the families could be punished by withholding privileges such as travel and business relationships. While perhaps unfair, such measures would be much less unfair than violence and much more acceptable in retrospect.

The remaining items in Table 5.1 are sufficiently straightforward that we need not elaborate upon them in text.

One striking feature in Table 5.1 is that many of the firm actions contemplated would need to be accomplished by others, notably Saudi, Egyptian, and other regional governments, although the same issues arise to lesser degree within friendly states such as Great Britain and Germany. Ultimately, it does not require brilliance to recognize the kinds of measures that could be applied and that might be effective. It is *practice*, rather than theory, that is difficult. Will the nations involved take the necessary steps at all? And if they do, how will they do it?

> Finding levers is the easy part. Causing ostensibly friendly heads of state to use them, and to do so reasonably, is hard.

America's allies in Europe began vigorous crackdowns immediately after September 11 and have reportedly cooperated closely with U.S. authorities. Both Egypt and Pakistan are increasingly doing so as well, although Pakistani President Musharraf clearly has very difficult political and internal-security challenges, and what will happen over the longer run remains to be seen.

CHALLENGES IN U.S.-SAUDI RELATIONS

Shared Interests but Competing Ideologies

Saudi Arabia is a unique and complicated case. On the one hand, the United States and Saudi Arabia have long had a strong and mutually beneficial strategic relationship. The two nations continue to have shared interests, and Saudi Arabia has even been attempting to help resolve the Israeli-Palestinian problem with a plan put forward by heir apparent Abdullah. On the other hand, the Saudi-supported spread of religious fundamentalism is a root problem:

> Internationally, the Saudis, both government-sponsored organizations and wealthy individuals, have exported a puritanical and at times militant version of Wahhabi Islam to other countries and communities. . . . Wealthy businessmen in Saudi Arabia, both members of the establishment and outsiders such as Osama bin Laden, have provided financial support to extremist groups who follow a militant fundamentalist brand of Islam with its Jihad culture.[10]

"Wahhabiism" (a shorthand term for something very complex)[11] is characterized as ultraconservative, puritanical, literalist, rigid, and intolerant; Wahhabis seek to *impose* their beliefs (Esposito, 2002, p. 106). It is not surprising that such teachings have sometimes mutated into an even more militant and virulent form—bin Laden's religious faith and sense of history apparently owe much to his study of Wahhabiism while he was a student (Esposito, 2002, p. 6), although other influences worked on him as well.

Ironically, although acceptance of the Wahhabi religious vision has long been a source of the Saudi government's religious and political legitimization (Esposito, 2002, p. 6; Ibrahim, 2002), Wahhabiism is not well accepted within Saudi Arabia itself:

> The alliance between the House of Saud—wealthy, cosmopolitan, and increasingly Western in tastes and habits—and the proponents of an austere form of Islam based on a literal interpretation of the Koran is becoming harder to sustain. . . .

---

[10]Esposito (2002, p. 49).

[11]Some of the Islamist movements treated with the catch-all Wahhabi label actually owe at least as much to other ideologies from Egypt and elsewhere as to true Saudi Wahhabiism, which is typically more conservative than revolutionary (Esposito, 2002, p. 111; Ibrahim, 2002). That the extremists do not in fact share a single "ism" is significant. Ayman al-Zawahiri, for example, came through the Muslim Brotherhood and Islamic Jihad of Egypt. He is sometimes described as providing greater theological depth than bin Laden himself (Mir, 2001).

Regional leaders and Saudi officials are daring to speak up against the backwards "Wahabi" vision of society. And Persian Gulf governments are taking a tougher line against extremists once thought to be useful, or at least relatively harmless. Instead of representing growing Wahabi power, the Sept. 11 attacks and their aftermath in Afghanistan may signal the peak. . . . The Wahabi outlook is detested by the Saudi ruling elite, the growing middle class and the vast powerful business communities.[12]

The situation, then, is complex. Nonetheless, if ideology is a major root cause for terrorism, it is desirable for the Saudis to do more than they have previously done to restrain and soften the nature of what is taught in the schools they support.[13] Further, it is desirable for the Saudis to work aggressively and cooperatively with the United States in combating terrorism in general and al Qaeda in particular.

The Next Steps

Reports differ widely on the degree to which Saudi Arabia has addressed the counterterrorism problem and cooperated with the United States. The Saudis have recently begun some crackdowns, and it is difficult to know what is being done behind the scenes, but, as noted above, it would seem that the Saudi government could do much more than it has so far to restrain and control objectionable ideological teachings and support (even indirect support) of foreign organizations that in turn support terrorism. Doing so might require a difficult confrontation with extremist components of the kingdom's fundamentalist religious establishment, who have long enjoyed considerable autonomy, but it is feasible, especially if Ibrahim's (2002) interpretation of circumstances is correct.

Some observers are quite pessimistic about improved U.S.-Saudi cooperation, while others are optimistic. We tend to be-

---

[12]Ibrahim (2002).

[13]The teaching of intolerance and hatred in the Saudi Islamic Academy in the Washington, DC, area recently became an issue because of a *Washington Post* report (Strauss and Wax, 2002).

lieve that the Saudi royal family and the United States have more basis for such cooperation than is widely recognized. In addition to the continued validity of the long-standing U.S.-Saudi strategic partnership regarding oil, the royal family probably understands that it is the ultimate target of al Qaeda, which has focused on the West for reasons that include a belief that the current governments of the Middle East would quickly topple if the United States were forced to back away. The Saudis may also be concerned that the Afghan campaign caused by the September 11 attacks and concern about Iraq have caused the United States to greatly *increase* its activities in the region (although not in the Gulf), which it finds inherently uncomfortable. And, as discussed above, some believe that the tide is turning against extremist sentiment. At the same time, the United States is rethinking the forces it needs in Saudi Arabia itself and thus potentially has something to offer. The time may be propitious, then, for the United States to prevail upon the Saudis to proceed more aggressively and to cooperate more fully. Many other issues exist that have to be worked simultaneously (e.g., the Israeli-Palestinian problem). As always in U.S.-Saudi relations, matters are complicated.

However that may be, if the influence component of counterterrorism strategy is to be taken seriously, the United States must prevail upon the Saudis to act forcefully, comprehensively, and cooperatively in ways that appear to be within their capability. Some of this will involve changes in ideological emphasis.

THE PAKISTAN PROBLEM

There are those who appear to espouse the notion that it would be a shame (although not a catastrophe for the United States) if President Musharraf were to fail, but when all is said and done, Pakistan is a declining asset. We would argue to the contrary that

- If Pakistan should fall to Islamist extremists (the most likely alternative to Musharraf), this might very well change regional perceptions of who is winning, restore credibility to causes such as that of al Qaeda, and reverse some of the gains made by Operation Enduring Freedom.

Thus, we believe that America's stake in Pakistan's political development is higher than many consider it to be.

BALANCING INTERESTS: *REALPOLITIK* VERSUS IDEALISM

One of the most difficult issues for strategy is that of balancing conflicting values and interests. There is a chronic conflict between maintaining the cooperation of Arab heads of state (Abdullah, Mubarak, etc.), favoring stability (at least avoiding chaotic and violent change), and promoting democracy.

This balancing problem was a matter of continuing debate within the project team during our research. In part, this reflected a generation gap, but it was mostly due to the fact that some of the scholars were much more sensitive than others to the extent of "democratic" currents within the Islamic world, currents commented upon by reporters and regional experts who travel within the region and talk (often in Arabic) to ordinary people rather than officials. Even the Islamists, who are typically vilified and considered to be all alike in U.S. discussions, are actually a complex mixture of individuals with highly varied views.

It can be argued that the United States has tilted too far in recent years to support stability in the Middle East and discourage the rise of Islamist parties, doing so at the expense of the U.S. belief in democracy. This view holds that the best thing that could happen in the Middle East is more democratization, even if it means the risk of temporary control by radical Islamists. Proponents of this view argue that the incompetence of the zealots would soon be evident and that moderation would follow. This theme has been debated for some time in the scholarly literature.[14]

We are not convinced by the arguments, but we take them seriously. It does seem to us that rebalancing and tempering is

---

[14]See Gerges (1999), which compares the views of "confrontationalist" and "accommodationist" scholars such as Bernard Lewis, Graham Fuller, and John Esposito.

needed. Nonetheless, our bottom line is that the U.S. priority should be destroying al Qaeda and, as a related matter, working the Israeli-Palestinian issue. Working with the heads of state (and leaning on them, as described earlier) is essential, however distasteful some aspects of their societies and policies continue to be. This is not the time to indicate any lack of political support. That said, it is important to be laying the groundwork for democratization now so that better choices will be available in the years ahead. Past history would indicate that the choices in ten years will be all too similar to today's, with the Middle East being no more democratic than it is now. It is beyond the scope of our effort to make detailed suggestions about how to avoid perpetuating the dilemma, but expressing our concern and making some observations is not.

What might be done? A start may be to recognize that in years past, the United States has not tried seriously to hold Middle Eastern states to the same standards of democratization as it has other nations. The time has come to begin doing so, although it will not be something to accomplish overnight. The United States has a variety of instruments to use for this purpose. One is to increase moral and fiscal support of UN organizations and NGOs that work to create the infrastructure of civil society, which has been notoriously difficult in the Middle East.[15] The U.S. State Department could do a good deal more if asked to do so. Prescriptions on such matters lie well outside the scope of our work, but we believe that it is possible both to work effectively with current leaders and to increase U.S. encouragement of democratization.

> Is the groundwork being laid so that the dilemma will be lessened in another 10 years?

UPHOLDING AMERICAN VALUES IN THE WAR AGAINST AL QAEDA

A particularly difficult and sensitive issue concerns whether it is feasible to uphold American values (or at least the traditional

---

[15]For an unusual discussion of such issues by a journalist, see Shadid (2002).

values of America at war) while conducting war against al Qaeda. The angry American man or woman in the street on September 12 might have regarded *any* retaliation as acceptable—some usually liberal-minded people were even calling for massive bombing such as that inflicted upon Germany and Japan in World War II—but it is essential that U.S. actions reflect the core values of the nation.

Avoiding simplistic one-liners such as "We must take the gloves off" is important because such glib remarks suppress real thought and abdicate control. "Getting tough" is not synonymous with brutality. Contrast the raping and pillaging by armies that was common in early history with the much more controlled use of force by Frederick the Great's professional army and many armed forces since.[16] Even Sherman's march to the sea—although considered brutal by the South—was controlled so as to avoid killing civilians. The damage inflicted was largely to property and economic productivity in direct support of the war effort.

A useful step in going beyond slogans is to seek distinctions that increase operating space (a general theme of this monograph). The conflicts between necessity and virtue can often be resolved if one merely looks for ways to do so. As a rule of thumb, the United States should generally deplore and work against certain classes of *actions* (most notably the killing of innocent civilians, but also, for example, international acts of terrorism involving diplomatic targets or transportation systems). This is in contrast to condemning and "declaring war" on all who use one or another form of terrorism in their political struggles. In this regard, we should distinguish between making war on al Qaeda and more generally combating terrorism. Terrorism is often intimately linked with resistance and rebellion. However much we may deplore various actions, it is not in the U.S. interest to automatically accept that another nation's troublesome terrorists are America's problem. To do so would *reduce* operating space and force the United States al-

---

[16]See Carr (2002) for an interesting discussion of such matters. Carr asserts (although other historians disagree) that terrorism against civilians has never worked in the long run.

ways to side with current heads of state against any rebellious faction that uses terror.

Another important step is to recognize that while American values in war applaud decisiveness and tolerate collateral damage, they also demand discriminate use of force in the large. There have been apparent exceptions (e.g., firebombings and the use of atomic weapons in World War II), but these occurred only in most unusual circumstances, and they were intensely controversial then and remain so.[17]   American values in war recognize the need for reduced levels of proof before action and the potential for mistakes, but arrogance and incompetent choices are another matter.[18]

Options for the current information war (closely related to political warfare) are particularly divisive.   Everyone understands that information war is crucial and American values in war have long embraced it.   However, the tradition is one of helping the information market work by disseminating truthful information, while avoiding the loss of integrity that occurs when lies are told (except tactically, as in confusing enemy communications or turning enemies against each other).   Lying to Congress and the public is strongly proscribed.   Although deceptions have sometimes been deemed necessary and have sometimes been tolerated, the value system requires that they be temporary, minimized, and controlled.

---

[17]Our point is not to second-guess decisions made during a world war 60 years ago, but to note that those U.S. (and allied) actions have been interpreted as "terrorism" by many scholars worldwide.   After all, the attacks had the explicit purpose of instilling terror in the civilian population and turning the people against their governments.   For an extensive bibliography and selections from the World War II debate by figures such as General Eisenhower, Admiral Leahy, Admiral Nimitz, General LeMay, and General MacArthur, see http://www.colorado.edu/AmStudies/lewis/2010/atomicdec.htm and http://www.douglong.com/ga1.htm.

[18]Although the issue is still debated, the U.S. destruction of a pharmaceutical plant in Sudan in 1998 is regarded by many to have been a blunder.   See Sheila MacVicar, "Blinded by Bad Science," ABC News, February 10, 1999 (available at http://abcnews.go.com/onair/DailyNews/wnt990210_sudan.html.)   The United States eventually released impounded funds of the plant's owner, and this was widely interpreted as the government admitting error.

In the case of internal matters, there is a long American history of extraordinary measures taken during times of war. Some have later been repudiated (e.g., the treatment of Japanese Americans during World War II). The fundamental values here are civil liberties such as due process and the search for speedy justice. Our views on these issues are rather conservative. We might endorse *more*-draconian measures than have yet been proposed in some areas (e.g., appointing counsel of the government's choice), and we are not reluctant to benefit from the less-constrained powers of allied police forces and the modified laws and procedures that have proved necessary in Britain, France, Germany, and Italy.[19]   However, locking people up— especially American citizens and noncitizens in the United States who have committed no serious crimes on the say-so of prosecutors, and then maintaining such prisoners indefinitely in isolation, without counsel, seems far beyond the pale. What is really happening on such matters cannot be judged today because of secrecy, but some of it will likely prove to have been outrageous when the history is written.[20]

> Speedy justice, yes, but that requires appropriately adapted due process and related protections.

Analytically, the tactic of long incarceration in solitary confinement is seldom effective in breaking the will of those with important knowledge. Thus, it violates rights but accomplishes little. What could be accomplished if lie detector tests could be required, if other nonlethal measures could be applied temporarily for screening purposes, or if illegal émigrés and their families were shipped back to countries with fewer procedural constraints? Changes of law would likely improve the ability to balance war needs and concern for civil rights, but the information needed to assess such changes is not available.

Finally, assuring press access has historically proved important. It improves faith in the government's integrity and avoids

---

[19]Some of these are discussed in an unpublished 1989 RAND study by Bruce Hoffman, Jennifer Duncan, and Jeffrey Simon, "U.S. Countermeasures Against Terrorism."

[20]See also National Commission on Terrorism (2000).

dangerous rumors, yet it conveys a sense of the ugliness inherent in war. Israel suffered badly in the recent information war when the press, having no access, began trumpeting stories of a possible massacre in Jenin, a massacre that apparently did not occur. Indeed, the Israeli army generally went to great lengths to avoid civilian casualties.[21]

---

[21] Moore (2002).

Chapter Six

CONCLUSIONS AND RECOMMENDATIONS

THE STORY IN BRIEF

It could be argued that September 11 was a colossal failure of deterrence. Although we have very little knowledge of al Qaeda's decisionmaking, we know that its leaders characterized the United States as weak, ineffective, and vulnerable (Schachter, 2002); and it seriously contemplated "defeating" the United States—forcing it to withdraw from the land of Muhammad and causing it great trouble by damaging the U.S. economy. Since September 11, there has been no public evidence to suggest that al Qaeda has been deterred by subsequent events. Is this surprising? Not really. History tells us that terrorists of this ilk seem not to be deterrable.

To make things worse, al Qaeda's leaders appear to have discounted plausible responses to their attacks. As a result, the kinds of actions that might theoretically be effective against al Qaeda are unthinkable, given American values—even American values in total war.

But wait. This does not mean what it may appear to mean. Facile language can disguise crucial distinctions: Even if the terrorists are not generally deterrable, specific terrorist *actions* may be deterrable even today. We know empirically that terrorists feel constraints, that they argue and plot among themselves, review and adapt strategies, worry about their perceived constituencies, and sometimes back away from tactics that seem to have gone too far. Similarly, we know that terrorists—even zealots—pay attention to and dislike operational risks.

Committed terrorists do not reform, but they do change actions, and that can be important.

In addition, what does the name "al Qaeda" mean? Even if al Qaeda's *leaders* (the usual implicit meaning of "al Qaeda") are not generally deterrable, what about others in the overall system that the organization comprises? We know that supporters of terrorists, for example, can often be deterred. The al Qaeda system, then, is not a single entity with an on-off switch.

Moreover, U.S. actions and threats against both state and non-state supporters will likely help deter other organizations, even if the only way to deal with al Qaeda itself is to destroy it.

Consider next the biggest concern of all, the specter of truly catastrophic terrorism, most likely through the use of WMD. Is this an event that can still be deterred? We suggest two possible approaches:

- Draw a line and credibly announce that anyone crossing that line by possessing or supporting the acquisition of WMD for terrorist purposes will be pursued relentlessly— forever, if necessary—with all the means necessary and with the United States willing to lower its standards of evidence, presume guilt, violate sovereignty, attack preemptively, and so on. Since the United States has essentially concluded that the line has already been crossed, there is little more to call upon for deterring al Qaeda, but U.S. actions in this regard—if pursued consistently and relentlessly—will surely help to deter supporters and other organizations.

- For the special and frightening case of biological weapons, deterrence could be greatly enhanced if everyone in the Middle East believed that a biological attack on the United States would inevitably lead to the spread of disease in the Middle East, where it could not possibly be contained and would destroy huge segments of the population. No threats in this regard are necessary (or desirable), but discussion is. A step in this direction would be to encourage recognition that infectious diseases (e.g., smallpox) would spread rapidly across borders because of international travel.

Finally, it is essential to understand that a strategy of *deterrence* is the wrong concept—it is both too limiting and too naive. It is far better to conceive a strategy with an *influence* component, which has both a broader range of coercive elements and a range of plausible positives, some of which we know from history are essential for long-term success.

NEXT STEPS FOR RESEARCH

Any project like the one summarized in this monograph uncovers many additional issues worthy of more research or follow-up action. We believe that research on the following would be particularly useful:

1. Planning and implementing political warfare.

2. Better understanding the actual decisionmaking of al Qaeda and other important terrorist organizations. Such research could identify points of internal dissension, relationships to the expressed views of state and spiritual leaders, and sensitivity to grass-roots opinion. It could identify fissures and points of leverage, as well as develop a framework for intelligence analysis and political warfare.

3. Better understanding how the U.S. government can create incentives for business and developers of infrastructure to emphasize flexibility, adaptiveness, and recoverability; and research on ways to communicate the robustness and readiness of the United States to retaliate, thereby disillusioning those who would seek to literally "bring the United States down."

4. Theory, doctrine, and rules of engagement to guide distributed counterterrorism groups *and* technology, organizations, and decision support to facilitate informed but rapid centralized decisions when those are necessary.

5. Operationalizing the influence component of strategy. This should involve a combination of regional studies by experts who are personally familiar with the language and culture of the Arab Middle East.

6. Strategies-to-tasks analysis to support the Office of Homeland Defense, the DoD, and the Department of Justice in understanding the influence component of strategy and its linkages to more direct offensive and defensive actions. The purpose of this analysis, as in traditional DoD work, would be to map high-level objectives into a hierarchy of increasingly detailed missions and tasks.

7. Portfolio-management analysis to assist various offices in resource allocation, drawing upon methods that have proven useful in work for the DoD and various social-policy domains.

8. The influence component of counterterrorism against organizations other than al Qaeda, including potential coercive actions that might be effective against Iraq, a next Serbia, or North Korea.

9. Sharpening our understanding of the relationships among terrorism, Islam, the political culture of Arab states, economic development, and political issues such as those relating to Israel and Palestine.

COLD WAR CONCEPTS OF DETERRENCE

Although the relatively simple concept of nuclear deterrence often associated with Bernard Brodie and Mutual Assured Destruction has not proven applicable in our study, actual U.S. Cold War deterrent strategy was much more sophisticated and nuanced, and many of its elements carry over, at least to some degree.

The deterrent value of uncontrollability (Schelling, 1960). Both the United States and the Soviet Union went to some lengths during the Cold War to remind each other that in the event of war, developments might get out of control despite best efforts.[1] The potential for full-scale general nuclear war was real and awesome, especially since both sides had honed their armed forces to fight such a nuclear war. A rough analog in the current era may be that if terrorists open the door to biological warfare, they should not imagine that there will be sanctuary or that their own people (i.e., those in the countries from which they come) will be spared. Infectious diseases would quickly cross borders and it would seem inevitable that at some point retaliation in kind would occur, even if no civilized country currently has plans and capabilities for such retaliation.

Flexible response (Schlesinger, 1973). The concept of flexible response moved the United States away from dependence on

---

[1]Examples of this can be found in Brown (1983) and Sokolovskii (1975). That Sokolovskii's book was ultimately about deterrence was discussed provocatively by Leites (1992).

massive retaliation as the sole deterrent. It was an essential development once the Soviet Union was able to credibly threaten massive retaliation on the United States while simultaneously threatening or even attacking Western Europe.

Identifying what the enemy values. An important theme dating from the mid-1970s consisted of determining what the Soviet Union's leaders held dear and "holding it at risk," a euphemistic way of saying that in the event of an attack on the United States, whatever the Soviet leaders valued (rather than what U.S. system analysis might imagine they *should* value) would be destroyed. Nuclear targeting, then, might have the objective of destroying the communist party's control structure, not just destructive devices such as missiles. Targeting might include attacks on the leaders themselves, even if they were in deep underground shelters.[2]

The countervailing strategy (Slocombe, 1981). Built on the theme of attacking what the Soviet leaders valued most, the countervailing strategy emphasized deterrence by denial, that is, convincing Soviet leaders that under no circumstances could they expect to win a nuclear war with the United States— as they themselves would judge "winning." Not only would they assuredly suffer massive retaliation if the United States chose to respond in that way, they would also fail to achieve their military objectives or end up with a usable power advantage— regardless of the level of nuclear activity. At the same time, the strategy was careful to avoid language that could be interpreted as promoting a warfighting, war-winning ambition.

Discriminate deterrence (Commission on Integrated Long-Term Strategy, 1987). The concept of discriminate deterrence emphasized threatening the opponent's valued possessions without necessitating broad violence that would cause innocents to suffer. This concept was motivated by both philosophy

---

[2]The Nuclear Targeting Policy Review was a major study, led by Leon Sloss and concluded in 1978, that incorporated many of the ideas mentioned here, building on work begun in the Ford administration and continued through the Carter administration. The related Presidential Directive, PD-59, was issued in July 1980.

and newly emerging capabilities of precision conventional munitions. It allowed for use of "stilettos" rather than "meat cleavers," had the potential for bcing more consistent with U.S. values, and was claimed to have the potential for greater credibility because it focused efforts at a level of violence to which the opponent could not respond effectively.

SELECTED DEFINITIONS

Dictionary definitions proved disappointing in our study because the stated meanings did not have the nuances that we required. Therefore, we adopted the following definitions:

Terrorism: violence committed or credibly threatened by groups in order to create fear and alarm within a population, either to cause a government to grant terrorists' demands or to otherwise achieve political objectives.

Co-opt: to influence an individual by bringing him into a group and thereby giving him a stake in the group's outcome.

Positively induce: to influence an individual by offering him something positive.

Persuade: to influence an individual by logical and emotional argument, as in going through pros and cons or appealing to values. (No assumption is made about prior leanings.)

Dissuade: to turn an individual from a course of action by persuasion, such as convincing him that his intended course would be unwise. (No assumption is made about threat per se.)

The definition of terrorism has been discussed and debated at length elsewhere (e.g., Hoffman, 1999; Pillar, 2001). The enduring dilemma is that some of those regarded by historians or dictionaries as terrorists have had understandable motivations, such as rebelling against repression. The old cliché "One man's terrorist is another man's freedom fighter" has considerable basis. Nonetheless, just as it has proven possible within military affairs to evolve a body of international law that prohibits some *actions* in war, it would seem possible to evolve a body of norms against some terrorist *actions*. In particular, violence against civilians is prohibited in war, although it is recognized that some unintended collateral damage will occur. The same should reasonably be true in nonwar settings such as those that pertain to terrorism. However, no consensus on this is likely soon, as can be seen in the widespread refusal of Palestinians to condemn the tactic of suicide bombing against quintessentially innocent Israeli citizens.

METHODS FOR ANALYZING COUNTERTERRORISM IN A COMPLEX ADAPTIVE SYSTEM

COMPLEX ADAPTIVE SYSTEMS

Terrorism typically occurs within what has come to be called a complex adaptive system (CAS). A CAS is characterized by dynamics, entities that affect each other directly and indirectly, the adaptation of those entities in response to developments, and recognizably different and important levels of phenomena (see, e.g., Holland, 1995). The evolution of a CAS can be exceedingly sensitive to initial conditions or "accidental" events along the way. In some circumstances, the course of events is completely unpredictable; however, it is sometimes possible to plan against alternative patterns of behavior. One can also plan for adaptivity (Davis, 2001, 2002a,b). A variety of methods are available for analyzing counterterrorism from a CAS perspective. We touch upon only a few here.

GAME-STRUCTURED ANALYSIS OF COMPLEX ADAPTIVE SYSTEMS

Complex adaptive systems that include thinking beings are especially interesting in that the behavior of those beings is in part a result of how their opponents (or allies) behave and in part the result of how they *believe* their opponents (or allies) will behave in the future and how they *believe* events will play out. Perceptions are critical. Figure C.1 is a schematic of a

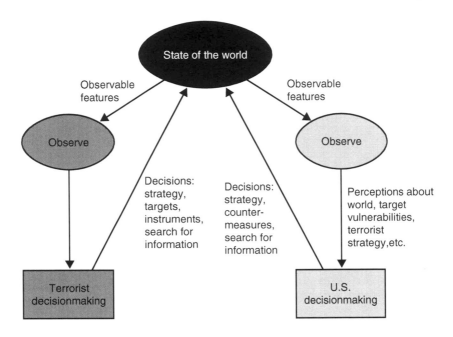

**Figure C.1—A Simple Game-Structured View
(simplified to a two–person game)**

simple two-party game-structured system, where Red is the terrorist group (see also National Research Council, 2002).

Figure C.2 points out that Red's decisions on what actions to take depend not only on its model of Blue (lower right-hand side of the figure), but also on the value it ascribes to the possible effects of its attacks on Blue, the availability of instruments, and so on. In rich applications of such work, the decisions of Red and Blue are complicated by random events occurring in the world and also their misperceptions about the world, their opponents, and the likely consequences of their actions.

The counterterrorism game should be conceived as having multiple players, including U.S. allies and terrorist supporters or suppliers. At higher levels of detail, there are subgroups, such as the relevant organs and departments of the U.S. gov-

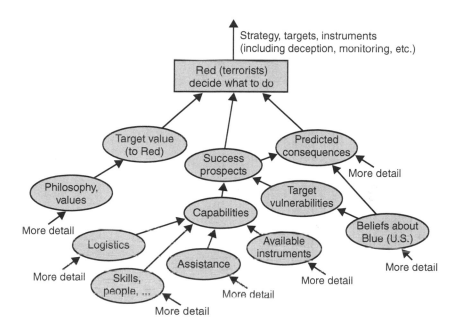

Figure C.2—Factors in Red's Decisions

ernment and the states, NGOs, and the business community. The presence of so many entities is one of the reasons that Red and Blue have difficulty making decisions: Cause and effect is often unclear, and both sides may be unaware of developments in train. Further, they often misunderstand each other.[1]

Another generalization of gaming is to *hypergames* (Bennett, 1980), in which the sides' objectives and measures of outcome are incommensurate: It is as though they are playing different games and not realizing it. Thus, a team may pursue an "optimal strategy," but in retrospect, it was for the wrong game. Such abstract theory may seem rather distant from developing a counterterrorism deterrent strategy, but those engaged in such development must consider these complications if they

_____

[1]See also the discussion in National Research Council (2002), which points to risk-analysis literatures as well as the methods discussed here.

are to make headway in understanding the terrorist mindset (or that of the other components of the terrorist system). This is all closely related, of course, to the well-understood need to recognize that elements of the terrorist systems do not think as we do—not for lack of rationality, but for other reasons. Both gaming and hypergaming may prove quite useful for expressing and debating such matters analytically.

SYNTHETIC COGNITIVE MODELING

Another technique for dealing with the problem of understanding one's opponent amid great uncertainty is to build alternative models that represent different but plausible reasoning patterns. This method has been applied in a number of instances over the past decade (National Research Council, 1997; Davis, 2002b) and shows considerable promise for counterterrorism as well. The models that appear to be most useful for decision support are simple enough in some respects to be discussed interactively with groups. Their purpose is largely to help defeat the "tyranny of the best estimate," which so often leads to policy-level errors. More generally, the models show promise for helping overcome well-known cognitive biases that affect decisionmaking (Jervis, 1976; Jervis, Lebow, and Stein, 1985; Axelrod, 1976).

ADAPTING THE CONSTRUCTS OF EFFECTS-BASED PLANNING

Much of the more-creative U.S. military planning in recent years has emphasized effects-based operations (EBO), that is,

> Operations conceived and planned in a systems framework that considers the full range of direct, indirect, and cascading effects—effects which may, with different degrees of probability, be achieved by the application of military, diplomatic, psychological, and economic instruments.[1]

Often, the purpose of EBO is to influence the behavior of adversaries—either individuals such as Saddam Hussein or groups such as al Qaeda. Influence on individuals is often described in terms such as *dissuade, deter,* or *compel.* Actions to influence groups may instead be described in terms such as *demoralization of an army* or *causing the collapse of support for the adversary's government.*

Many of EBO's constructs are applicable to counterterrorism. Although effects-based planning (EBP) was initially regarded by many observers as yet another fad, it is increasingly recognized as central to sound development of strategy. Moreover, it is no longer an abstraction. Not only did the United States practice EBO in the latter days of the war over Kosovo, Osama bin

---

[1]Davis (2001).

Laden and al Qaeda also practiced EBO against the United
States when they attacked the symbolic pillars of U.S. capital-
ism and military strength,[2] intentionally killing thousands of
innocents. Historians will argue for years about the effects on
Slobodan Milosevic of the pointed U.S. bombing that characterized the latter weeks of the Kosovo war, but no one can doubt
the effects on U.S. behavior of the September 11 attacks.
Those effects were in part intended by bin Laden (direct killing
and destruction, followed by America's shock as it recognized
that it was not a sanctuary), in part hoped-for (consternation
and enormous efforts to improve security), and in part a very
unpleasant surprise (the massive and relentless U.S. war
against al Qaeda and the Taliban in Afghanistan).

Effects-based operations operate in both physical and cognitive
domains (Figure D.1), although the ability to assess options is
strong only in the physical domain at present.

The following principles have been suggested for analysis in
support of EBO:

*   Confront uncertainty by assessing capabilities by their
    most likely, best-case, and worst-case outcomes. Alleged
    best-estimate assessments are unreliable, and focusing on
    them can both discourage actions that have enormous up-
    side potential and hide risks.

*   Use low-resolution exploratory analysis for breadth and
    more detailed modeling and gaming for both depth and in-
    sight into underlying phenomena.

*   Use qualitative modeling, including synthetic cognitive
    modeling of the decisionmaking and behavior of command-
    ers, political leaders, and even societies. Such modeling
    can enrich analysis and break down barriers between "rig-
    orous analysis" (usually quantitative, but rigid) and human
    gaming (often more realistic and innovative, but fuzzy).

---

[2]Bin Laden emphasized the iconic nature of the targets in an interview (Mir,
2001), where he characterized the killing of women and children as a regret-
table part of defensive jihad.

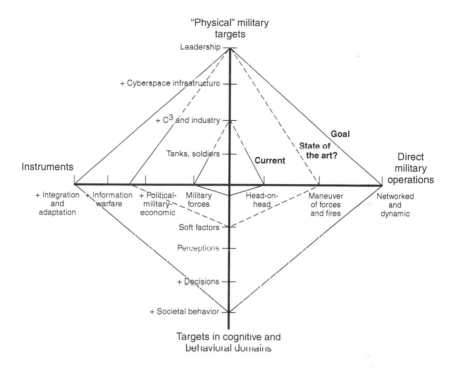

Figure D.1—Effects-Based Operations Operate in Physical and Cognitive Domains

- Organize modeling around adaptive systems for command and control and other matters, rather than around the mass and physical characteristics of forces. This implies emphasis on the concepts and technology of agent-based modeling, as well as on system engineering.

- Develop a new base of empirical information, including information obtainable from history and from a combination of gaming, man-in-the-loop simulation, and experiments.

BIBLIOGRAPHY

Alberts, David, John Garstka, and Frederick Stein (1999), *Network Centric Warfare: Developing and Leveraging Information Technology*, CCRP Publication Series, Department of Defense, Washington, DC.

Arquilla, John, and David Ronfeldt (eds.) (2001), *Networks and Netwars: The Future of Terror, Crime, and Militancy*, RAND, Santa Monica, CA.

Asprey, Robert B. (1994), *War in the Shadows: Guerrillas in History*, W. Morrow, New York, NY.

Axelrod, Robert (1976), *The Structure of Decision*, Princeton University Press, Princeton, NJ.

Bennett, Peter (1980), "Hypergames: Developing a Theory of Conflict," *Futures*, Vol. 12, pp. 489–507.

Bodansky, Yossef (1999), *Bin Laden: The Man Who Declared War on America, Forum*, Prima Publishing, Roseville, CA.

Bonoan, Rafael, Paul Davis, Brad Roberts, Victor Utgoff, and Caroline Ziemke (2002), *Deterring Terrorism: Exploring Theory and Methods*, Institute for Defense Analyses, Washington, DC, Paper P-3717, August.

Bremer, L. Paul (1998), Inteview on the News Hour, Public Broadcasting, August 25.

Brown, Harold (1983), *Thinking About National Security: Defense and Foreign Policy in a Dangerous World*, Westview Press, New York, NY.

Carr, Caleb (2002), *The Lessons of Terror: A History of Warfare Against Civilians: Why It Has Always Failed and Why It Will Fail Again*, Random House, New York, NY.

Commission on Integrated Long-Term Strategy (1987), *Discriminate Deterrence*, commission chaired by Fred C. Iklé and Albert Wohlstetter, Department of Defense, Washington, DC.

Dao, James (2002), "State Dept. Raises Concerns About Israel's Use of U.S.-Made Arms," *New York Times*, July 25.

Davis, Paul K. (ed.) (1994), *New Challenges in Defense Planning: Rethinking How Much Is Enough*, RAND, Santa Monica, CA.

Davis, Paul K. (1997), Appendix F of *Post-Cold War Conflict Deterrence*, Naval Studies Board, National Research Council, National Academy of Sciences, Washington, DC.

Davis, Paul K. (2001), *Effects-Based Operations: A Grand Challenge for the Analyltic Community*, RAND, Santa Monica, CA.

Davis, Paul K. (2002a), *Analytic Architecture for Capabilities-Based Planning, Mission-System Analysis, and Transformation*, RAND, Santa Monica, CA.

Davis, Paul K. (2002b), *Synthetic Cognitive Modeling for Effects-Based Planning, Proceedings of the SPIE*, Vol. 4716, April (to be published in late 2002).

Defense Science Board (1998), *Defense Science Board Summer Study Task Force on DoD Responses to Transnational Threats. Volume III: Supporting Reports*, Defense Science Board, Washington, DC.

Dror, Yehezkel (1980), *Crazy States: A Counterconventional Strategic Problem*, Heath Lexington Books, D.C. Heath and Co., Lexington, MA.

Dror, Yehezkel (1998), "Israel's Quest for Ultimate Security: Strategies and Perceptions," in Daniel Bar-Tal, Dan Jacobson, and Aharon Klieman (eds.), *Security Concerns: Insights from the Israeli Experience*, JAI Press, Stamford, CT.

Esposito, John L. (2002), *Unholy War: Terror in the Name of Islam*, Oxford, New York, NY.

George, Alexander L. (1980), *Presidential Decisionmaking in Foreign Policy: The Effective Use of Information and Advice*, Westview, Boulder, CO.

Gerges, Fawaz A. (1999), *America and Political Islam: Clash of Cultures or Clash of Interests*, Cambridge University Press, Cambridge, UK.

Hashim, Ahmed S. (2001), "The World According to Usama Bin Laden," Naval War College Review, Autumn, Vol. LIV, No. 4, pp. 11–36.

Hawley, Len (2002), "Generic Pol Mil Plan: Multilateral Complex Contingency Operation," unpublished paper, U.S. Department of State, Washington, DC.

Hersh, Seymour (1993), *The Samson Option: Israel's Nuclear Arsenal and America's Foreign Policy*, Vintage Books, London.

Higgins, Andrew, and Alan Cullison (2002), "Terrorist's Odyssey: Saga of Dr. Zawahiri," *Wall Street Journal*, July 2, p. A.1.

Hillestad, Richard, and Paul K. Davis (1997), *Resource Allocation in the New Defense Strategy: The DynaRank Decision Support System*, RAND, Santa Monica, CA.

Hoffman, Bruce (1999), "Old Madness, New Methods: Revival of Religious Terrorism Begs for Broader U.S. Policy," *RAND Review*, Winter, 1998-1999 (available at http://www.rand.org/publications/randreview/issues/rrwinter98.9.pdf).

Hoffman, Bruce (2001), "Rethinking Terrorism in Light of a War on Terrorism," testimony before the Subcommittee on Terrorism and Homeland Security, House Permanent Select Committee on Intelligence, September 26, 2001. Reprinted as CT-182, RAND, Santa Monica, CA (available at http://www.rand.org/publications/CT/CT182).

Holland, John (1995), *Hidden Order: How Adaptation Builds Complexity,* Addison-Wesley, Reading, MA.

Huntington, Samuel (1993), "The Clash of Civilizations?" *Foreign Affairs*, Vol. 22, Summer.

Huntington, Samuel (1997), *The Clash of Civilizations and the Remaking of World Order*, Simon and Schuster, New York, NY.

Ibrahim, Youssef (2002), "The Mideast Threat That's Hard to Define," *Washington Post*, August 11.

Iklé, Fred, and Albert Wohlstetter (co-chairmen) (1988), *Report of the Commission on Long-Term Integrated Strategy*, Department of Defense, Washington, DC.

Jehl, Douglas (2001), "A Nation Challenged: Saudi Arabia: Holy War Lured Saudis as Rulers Looked Away," *New York Times,* December 27.

Jenkins, Brian (2001), "Terrorism: Current and Long Term Threats," Congressional Testimony, Senate Armed Services Subcommittee on Emerging Threats, November 15, 2001. Reprinted as CT-187, RAND, Santa Monica, CA (available at www.rand.org/publications/CT/CT187/).

Jenkins, Brian Michael (2002), *Countering al Qaeda: An Appreciation of the Situation and Suggestions for Strategy*, RAND, Santa Monica, CA.

Jervis, Robert (1976), *Perception and Misperception in International Politics*, Princeton University Press, Princeton, NJ.

Jervis, Robert, Richard Ned Lebow, and Janice Gross Stein (1985), *Psychology and Deterrence*, Johns Hopkins Press, Baltimore, MD.

Kugler, Richard (1993), *Commitment to Purpose: How Alliance Partnership Won the Cold War*, RAND, Santa Monica, CA.

Lavoy, Peter R., Scott D. Sagan, and James J. Wirtz (2000), *Planning the Unthinkable: How New Powers Will Use Nuclear, Biological, and Chemical Weapons*, Cornell University Press, Ithaca, NY.

Leites, Nathan (1992), *Soviet Style in War*, RAND, Santa Monica, CA.

Lesser, Ian, Bruce Hoffman, John Arquilla, David Ronfeldt, Michele Zanini, foreword by Brian Jenkins (1999), *Countering the New Terrorism*, RAND, Santa Monica, CA.

Lewis, Bernard (2002), *What Went Wrong: Western Impact and Middle Eastern Response*, Oxford, London.

Lewis, Leslie, and Robert Roll (1993), *Strategies to Tasks: A Methodology for Resource Allocation and Management,* RAND, Santa Monica, CA, P-7839.

Mir, Hamid (2001), "Osama Claims He Has Nukes," Online at Dawn, Internet Edition, November 10, available at http://www.dawn.com/2001/11/10/top1.htm.

Moore, Molly (2002), "Jenin Camp Is a Scene of Devastation, But Yields No Evidence of Massacre," *Washington Post*, April 16, p. A1.

Mylroie, Laurie (2000), *Study of Revenge: Saddam Hussein's Unfinished War Against America*, American Enterprise Institute, Washington, DC.

National Commission on Terrorism (2000), *Countering the Changing Threat of International Terrorism,* Washington, DC.

National Research Council (1997), *Post-Cold War Conflict Deterrence*, Naval Studies Board, National Academy of Sciences, Washington, DC.

National Research Council (2000), *Network Centric Naval Forces*, National Academy Press, Washington, DC.

National Research Council (2002), *Making the Nation Safer: The Role of Science and Technology in Countering Terrorism* (the Branscomb/Klauser study), National Academy of Sciences, National Academy Press, Washington, DC.

Pillar, Paul R.(2001), *Terrorism and U.S. Foreign Policy,* Brookings, Washington, DC.

Pirnie, Bruce R. (1996), *An Objectives-Based Approach to Military Campaign Analysis*, RAND, Santa Monica, CA, MR-656.

Post, Jerrold M. (1999), "Psychological and Motivational Factors in Terrorist Decision-Making: Implications for CBW Terrorism," in Jonathan B. Tucker,. *Toxic Terror: Assessing Terrorist Use of Chemical and Biological Weapons*, MIT Press, Cambridge, MA.

Powers, Michael J. (2001), *Deterring Terrorism with CBRN Weapons: Developing a Conceptual Framework*, The Chemical and Biological Arms Control Institute (CBACI), Washington, DC, February, available at http://www.cbaci.org/deterringCBRNterrorism.pdf.

Quinlivan, James (1999), "Coup-Proofing: Its Practice and Consequences in the Middle East," *International Security*, Vol. 24, No. 2. Also available as RP-844, RAND, Santa Monica, CA.

Roberts, Brad (ed.) (1993), *Biological Weapons: Weapons of the Future?* The Center for Stategic and International Studies (CSIS), Washington, DC.

Roberts, Brad (1998), *Combating NBC Terrorism: An Agenda for Enhancing International Cooperation*, The Chemical and Biological Arms Control Institute (CBACI), Washington, DC.

Roberts, Brad (2002), *Deterring Terrorism: Terrorist Campaigns and Prolonged Wars of Mutual Coercion*, annotated version of a briefing given in May 2002, Institute for Defense Analyses, Arlington, VA.

Rumsfeld, Donald (2001), *Quadrennial Defense Review Report*, Department of Defense, Washington, DC, September.

"The Saudi-Terror Subsidy (2002)," *The Weekly Standard*, May 20.

Schachter, Jonathan (2002), "Deterring Al-Qa'Idah: Past, Present and Future," unpublished paper, RAND Graduate School, Santa Monica, CA.

Schelling, Thomas (1960), *The Strategy of Conflict*, Harvard University Press, Cambridge, MA (2d ed., 1980).

Schlesinger, James (circa 1973), *Annual Defense Report*, Department of Defense, Washington, DC.

Shadid, Anthony (2002), *Legacy of the Prophet: Despots, Democrats, and the New Politics of Islam*, Westview, Boulder, CO.

Slocombe, Walter (1981), "The Countervailing Strategy," *International Security*, Vol. 5, No. 4, Spring.

Sokolovskii, Vasilii Danilovich (1975), *Soviet Military Strategy*, 3d ed., MacDonald and Jane's, London.

Strauss, Valerie, and Emily Wax (2002), "Where Two Worlds Collide: Muslim Schools Face Tension of Islamac, U.S. Views," *Washington Post*, February 25, p. Aa.

Tucker, Jonathan B. (ed.) (1999), *Toxic Terror: Assessing Terrorist Use of Chemical and Biological Weapons*, MIT Press, Cambridge, MA.

United States Commission on National Security (1999), *New World Coming: Studies and Analysis*, Rudman-Hart Commission, Washington, DC.

United States Commission on National Security (2001), *Road Map for National Security: The Imperative for Change, Phase III Report*, Rudman-Hart Commission, Washington, DC.

Utgoff, Victor (2002), "Observations on the Problem of Deterring Terrorism," Final Briefing to DARPA, Institute for Defense Analyses, Arlington, VA.

Utgoff, Victor, and R. Bonoan (2002), "Components of a Strategic Approach to Deterring Terrorism," annotated version of a briefing given in May 2002, Institute for Defense Analyses, Arlington, VA.

Warner, Edward, and Glenn Kent (1984), *A Framework for Planning the Employment of Air Power in Theater War*, RAND, Santa Monica, CA, N-2038-AF.

Zeigler, Bernard P., Herbert Praehofer, and Tag Gon Kim (2000), *Theory of Modeling and Simulation,* 2d ed., *Integrating Discrete Event and Continuous Complex Dynamic Systems*, Academic Press, San Diego, CA.

Ziemke, Caroline F. (2002), "Deterring Terrorism: A Strategic Personalities Framework," annotated version of a briefing given in May 2002, Institute for Defense Analyses, Arlington, VA.

Ziemke, Caroline, Philippe Loustaunau, and Amy Alrich (2000), *Strategic Personality and the Effectiveness of Nuclear Deterrence*, Institute for Defense Analyses and Defense Threat Reduction Agency, D-2537.

PAUL K. DAVIS

Paul K. Davis is a research leader at RAND and a professor at the RAND Graduate School. His research has primarily been in the areas of defense planning, military transformation, more general strategic planning, psychology-informed deterrence theory, and advanced methods of analysis and modeling. He was a program manager at RAND from 1981 to 1990, and a corporate research manager from 1991 to 1996. He is a member of the Naval Studies Board under the National Research Council and has served on a number of studies for the Council and the Defense Science Board. He was the editor of RAND's 1994 book, *New Challenges for Defense Planning: Rethinking How Much Is Enough*, and he published a book on capabilities-based planning in 2002. Before joining RAND in 1981, he worked in the federal government from 1975 to 1981 during three administrations, becoming a senior executive in the Office of the Secretary of Defense in 1979 and an acting deputy assistant secretary in 1981. He received a distinguished civilian service medal for his work on policies and programs related to the Persian Gulf and what has become the U.S. Central Com mand. In earlier years, he worked on strategic nuclear issues and strategic technology. From 1971 to 1975 he was on the staff of the Institute for Defense Analyses. He holds a B.S. from the University of Michigan and a Ph.D. in Chemical Physics from the Massachusetts Institute of Technology.

BRIAN MICHAEL JENKINS

Brian Jenkins has served since 1998 as senior adviser to the president of RAND. He had been with RAND for some 20 years before leaving in 1989 to become Deputy Chairman of Kroll Associates, an international investigative and consulting firm. He is one of the world's leading authorities on international terrorism and serves as a consultant to numerous government agencies and major corporations.

From 1986 to 1989, he was chairman of RAND's Political Science Department and also directed RAND's research on political violence. A former captain in the elite Green Berets, he served in the Dominican Republic during the American intervention, and later in Vietnam (1966–1967), where he was decorated on several occasions for valor in combat. He returned to Vietnam in 1968 as a member of General Creighton Abrams' Long-Range Planning Task Group and was honored with the Department of the Army's highest award for his work there. He is the author of *International Terrorism: A New Mode of Conflict*, the editor and coauthor of *Terrorism and Personal Protection*, and a coauthor of *The Fall of South Vietnam* and *Aviation Terrorism and Security*. His most recent study, *Countering al Qaeda*, was published by RAND in 2002. He has contributed chapters to several other books on political violence and has published more than 100 RAND reports and papers, as well as numerous articles. In 1996, President Clinton appointed him to the White House Commission on Aviation Safety and Security. He also is a special advisor to the International Chamber of Commerce. In addition, he serves as chairman of the International Working Group on International Violence, a trans-Atlantic group involved in research on terrorism. He holds a B.A. in Fine Arts and an M.A. in History, both from the University of California, Los Angeles, and he has a postgraduate degree in Humanities from the University of San Carlos in Guatemala.